EMOTIONAL GAMES FOR TRAINING

EMOTIONAL GAMES FOR TRAINING

15 games that explore feelings, behaviour and values

KEN JONES

Gower

© Ken Jones 2002

The materials that appear in this book, other than those quoted from prior sources, may be reproduced for education/training activities. There is no requirement to obtain special permission for such uses.

This permission statement is limited to reproduction of materials for educational or training events. Systematic or large-scale reproduction or distribution – or inclusion of items in publication for sale – may be carried out only with prior written permission from the publisher.

Published by
Gower Publishing Limited
Gower House
Croft Road
Aldershot
Hants GU11 3HR
England

Gower
131 Main Street
Burlington VT 05401-5600 USA

Ken Jones has asserted his right under the Copyright, Designs and Patents Act 1988 to be identified as the author of this book.

British Library Cataloguing in Publication Data

Jones, Ken, 1923–
　Emptional games for training : 15 games that explore
　feelings, behaviour and values
　1. Employees – Training 2. Educational games 3. Emotions
　I. Title
　658.3'1244
　ISBN 0 566 08497 X

Library of Congress Control Number: 2001099783

Typeset by Wileman Design
Printed in Great Britain by T J International Ltd., Padstow, Cornwall

Contents

Introduction	vii
Emotional Word List	xix
Facilitator's Checklist	xxi
Emotional Games: Summary	xxiii
The Games and Simulations	1
1. Playing Games	3
2. About Face	13
3. Double Leap	25
4. Leisure	31
5. Planet Zita	39
6. Interest	59
7. Newsroom	67
8. Happiness Project	87
9. Secrecy	95
10. Creating Events	105
11. Feeling Virtuous	115
12. Boat Tax	123
13. Hunting Pink	133
14. Elite	143
15. Way Out	155
Other works by Ken Jones	163

Introduction

Emotions in business, as in life, are the tricky bits. They have a tendency to get out of hand, to take over. Or they get bottled up and explode later. Carefully devised plans which seem great on paper can become derailed by seemingly irrational emotions. This book contains games and simulations designed to provide practical experiences for understanding and handling emotions in the context of communication skills.

Philosophy of Emotions

Part of the problem with emotions is a simple misconception – perceiving *reason* and *emotion* as two incompatible states of mind. From this it is only a short step to think of emotions as non-rational and a further short step to assume they are irrational and unreasonable.

There is a tendency for planners to exclude emotional factors from their plans and then blame someone else when emotions undermine the project. This failure, of course, generates emotions in the minds of the planners and their bosses.

The philosophy behind this book is that emotions are often rational in the sense that they are based on what has happened in the past – the development of values, ethics, attitudes and behaviour – all involving rational thoughts.

To belittle emotions is to fail to understand them. This failure of understanding leads to inadequate responses that can make matters worse. For example, an outburst of anger tends to generate anger. This book provides scenarios that can produce spontaneous emotions which can then be explored in the debriefings – and not just the emotions themselves, but the thoughts and feelings behind them. Thoughts can trigger emotions and emotions can give rise to thoughts; the two are intertwined.

Fear is a key emotion. It comes in many forms – fear of speaking in public, fear of making a fool of oneself, fear of the boss and even fear of oneself. But the emotions and the personal values associated with the scenarios in this book are essentially professional – feelings involving honesty, courtesy, responsibility and even kindness. All the emotions, from love to hate, usually have a rational basis. They are not bolts from the blue; they arise because they are consistent with our personalities.

The events in this book are diverse and cover different sorts of rational emotion. Nor are the emotions confined to the subject matter, they are also present in the methodology. The emotions of games and simulations are different from those experienced when watching a

Introduction

video, listening to a lecture, writing an essay or sitting an examination. The emotions related to having power over events are very different from those of being under instruction.

Emotions, of course, are not always on display. Sometimes they are concealed. Nor is it easy for the participants themselves, let alone observers, to know what the emotions are. Despite these obvious difficulties it is usually worthwhile trying to become aware of the type of emotions that are being felt. In this respect a useful starting point could be the Emotional Word List which sets out 164 words which could answer the question 'How do you feel?'

Emotional Dangers

The events in this book are designed to promote awareness of emotions. In the 15 events no change of personalities is required – participants are not instructed to be loving or hostile, angry or peaceful. The emphasis is on professional behaviour and most of it is group behaviour – thus sheltering participants from being demonized as individuals.

Also avoided are any 'mish-mash' events, in which the participants do not know whether they are supposed to try to win or to try to behave professionally. In such events some people behave one way and some another without realizing that their motives are irreconcilable. This clash of methodologies is usually interpreted as a clash of personalities with the facilitator blaming the participants for the ill-feeling and the participants blaming each other. The emotional outcome can be serious and can often cause damage to reputations and friendships. (For actual examples of what can go wrong in games and simulations readers might care to look at my *Games and Simulations Made Easy*, Kogan Page, 1997.)

Emotional Games for Training avoids such a conflict by specifying the methodology of the event and describing the type of behaviour required. Thus, the emotions tend to be scenario-based – what people naturally feel when trying to win (as in a game) or when trying to behave professionally (as in a simulation).

Emotional Word List

The list of 164 words is not, of course, a list of emotions. It is a list of words that are related to feelings and could answer questions about how people feel.

Only a few of the Facilitator's Notes mention this list but it really is worthwhile keeping the list available when planning, briefing, running and debriefing. It can be particularly useful because emotions are an aspect of education and training that is often ignored or underplayed. Consequently, students and trainees become conditioned to respond only to the factual and intellectual

Introduction

aspects of subjects: they want the facts; they want to know the nature of the 'problems'. The procedures used in the worlds of business and education are similar – they are all designed for assessing the facts and solving problems. Teachers and trainers have the job of asking the questions and the students and trainees have the job of answering them.

This mind-set is a handicap in development and in life not because it is wrong but because it is limited. Human behaviour involves emotions. They are as inescapable as they are important.

The mind-set of intellectual problem-solving may indicate a desire to sanitize life. Hurt and distress, pain and anger can, it would seem, be banished by being converted into problems. Problems can be stated, problems can be analysed and problems can be solved and then everything will be all right – at least, that is the implication.

The purpose of the Emotional Word List is to help people break free from the problem-solving mind-set. Not only are emotions inevitable and important, they should be recognized and understood. And this is not merely another way of gaining knowledge, it is also an affirmation of humanity.

Games and Simulations

Games and simulations are untaught events. Their function is to give power to the participants who must be allowed to make their own mistakes. There is no place for a teacher, trainer, tutor or instructor in games and simulations. The trainer becomes the facilitator who is in charge of the mechanics of the event but has no role in trying to nudge the participants into making sensible decisions or finding the 'right' answers. A game or simulation in which participants make mistakes and errors of judgement is not a failed event; it is probably a highly successful event in terms of learning from experience.

Advice

All the events in this book include Facilitator's Notes and Notes for Participants which explain the nature of the event and the 'rules'. As far as possible these 'rules' are plausible constraints within the scenario – business, government, management and so on.

The Facilitator's Notes contain advice about how to handle the timing and location of the event and suggestions for those events which require groups. (In general I advise that groups should be selected on a random basis. It is preferable that people should try to work together rather than form cliques.) The Notes contain sections dealing with the preparations for the event, the briefing, the action and the debriefing. Of these, the debriefing is probably the most important. It is crucial not to allow the event itself to over-run so that sufficient time remains for a debriefing.

Introduction

The Notes for Participants contain an outline of the event and mention any relevant constraints. They also make the methodology clear. These Notes should be handed out at the start of the briefing and then retrieved before the action in order to avoid inappropriate items in the action area. Unlike identity cards and form sheets, the Notes for Participants have no place within the action of the event.

Psychology, Ethics and Values

What I have not dealt with in much detail is advice which would normally come under the heading of psychology – the best way to relieve stress, the importance of self-awareness, the value of motivation, the need for empathy, leadership and so on. Such topics are touched on only as possible lines of exploration in the debriefings, depending on the way things work out in the actual events. There are plenty of textbooks available in these subject areas.

Similarly, I have deliberately limited my comments on ethics and values, apart from alerting the facilitator to the opportunities. Such matters are best left to the facilitator and the participants, depending on the nature of the course and what happens in the events themselves.

Psychology, ethics and values are, of course, causes of emotions. They are part of one's personality and they are a starting point in any behavioural activity. Similarly, the 15 games and simulations in the book should also be regarded as starting points. They do not determine the finishing points. Their open-ended nature allows many possible destinations.

Adaptability

All the events should be regarded as adaptable. For example, an event could be allowed to continue into another session, despite having a debriefing. The starting point for the next session could be where the event ended. Alternatively, a resumed event might continue but with a change of roles or rules.

Such re-runs can be highly effective in allowing participants to look at the situation from a different perspective. Moreover, they give the participants an opportunity to improve their actions. Saying 'I didn't repeat that mistake' is far more satisfying than thinking 'I'll try not to repeat that mistake should such a situation arise again.' Learning from experience is far more effective if it can be demonstrated that the experience has been learned.

Adaptations should not go so far as to change the methodology. For example, if anger is a topic in the syllabus, some participants might be told not to behave professionally but to play-act anger or some other emotion. This changes the methodology from game or simulation to drama and play-acting.

Characteristics

Apart from aiming to provide experience in emotions in the context of communication skills there are two other characteristics worth noting.

The first is that, apart from the Planet Zita simulation, there are no 'right' answers. The aim is not to learn facts, or even to solve problems, but to understand and appreciate behaviour, including the emotions that are implicit in that behaviour. It is the understanding that is the first step.

It follows from this that, if participants ask 'Have we got the answer right?', then they have misunderstood the nature of the event. The aims, action and the debriefing are concerned with feelings and behaviour. An advantage of having no 'right' answers is the removal of a good deal of the fear of getting it wrong. Of course, there are ways of doing things better that can be explored in the debriefing, but most of the issues are matters of opinion. Opinions can differ without being classified as right or wrong. The events are concerned with values, ethics and emotions. These are the foundations of our characters and philosophies; they are central to ourselves.

The second characteristic is fiction. All the scenarios deal with imaginary countries, institutions and societies. The assumption is that the Republic of Alpha – the location of most scenarios – is a democracy with similar laws and customs and ethics to those we are accustomed to. For the participants, the advantages of fiction are as follows:

1. They do not have to learn a mass of factual details before entering the action.
2. They are not tempted to imitate the real world rather than making their own decisions.
3. They can speak out freely without the fear that someone will say, 'You've made a mistake.' The aim is not to learn facts but to communicate.

With fiction one can strip away all irrelevancies in order to concentrate on those aspects that are the most appropriate and, on occasions, produce extreme cases in order to illuminate points of principle.

These characteristics – no right answers and fictional scenarios – help facilitators and participants understand emotions.

Reality

It is possible to argue that, since the scenarios are fictitious, the events themselves are unreal. A participant might ask, 'Why do we have to waste our time on these games and simulations? Why not deal with the real world?'

The simple answer is that the important aspect is behaviour and

Introduction

that the behaviour is real. The participants do not play-act, they try to understand what is going on and to communicate effectively. Experience of such events soon demonstrates this reality – there are real plans, real initiatives, real communications and real emotions. Of course, the participant (manager, customer, television producer) has a fictitious (and unpaid!) role, but their behaviour is not fictitious. Only the scenario is simulated – the thoughts, emotions and actions are real. Thus the events generate real self-awareness, real empathy and real understanding.

In addition, the experiences are far wider than is possible in real life. Taking part in several of these events creates a variety of situations and responsibilities which help participants develop behaviour that is applicable in the real world of responsibilities, ideas and emotions. As such, these are real experiences as distinct from imagining how one might behave in that situation.

Preliminaries

Start with your own emotions. These are extremely important. Go through the Emotional Word List and select three or four that match your feelings. If you select such words as 'enthusiastic' and 'confident' you are probably experienced and know what to do and how to do it. Even so, it is worthwhile looking at the advice in the Facilitator's Checklist about briefing, running and debriefing these events. If your selected words include 'worried' or 'apprehensive' then you should seek reassurance by involving colleagues and/or some of the participants themselves. For example, run Planet Zita on your own, cutting out the map squares and putting yourself into the roles of the five members of the space crew. Or, better still, run it with your family, friends or colleagues. Indeed, with any of the 15 events you can imagine yourself in a role and decide what you would do and what would be likely to happen as a result.

Whether you are confident or apprehensive, consider appointing one or two participants to help brief, run and debrief these events. You could ask for volunteers, choose randomly or make your own selection. These assistant facilitators can probably anticipate their colleagues' reactions better than you can. Show them the materials, including the Emotional Word List and the Facilitator's Checklist. You may be surprised by their helpful suggestions. Delegating authority gives you a better opportunity to monitor what occurs, as well as supporting the methodology.

If you run several games or simulations it might be possible to allow participants to take it in turns to brief, run and debrief.

Finally, bear in mind the possibility of re-running the event. Participants usually welcome the chance to do better next time.

Tripwires for the Facilitator

It is not unknown for a game or simulation to come unstuck because some simple precaution was not taken. The following guidelines will help minimize this possibility:

- Check carefully that you are equipped with the required materials before you start the briefing. Arriving without the Notes for Participants or without one important Knowledge Card will be disastrous.
- Look carefully to see whether the event should have any unusual artefacts – for example, a 'Talking Rod' in Leisure or an adequate supply of marbles, rulers, coloured pens, and so on in Double Leap.
- Think about the personalities of the participants. Although I generally recommend that roles be allocated at random there can be situations where it might be better to ask for volunteers for a particular job.
- Remember to keep to a consistent vocabulary. Avoid calling a simulation a game or vice versa. Try to avoid a hyphenated label such as 'simulation-game'. Using a floating vocabulary can confuse participants as to whether they are supposed to play to win in the magic kingdom of a game or whether they are expected to behave professionally as in real life.
- These 15 events are very motivational and it is, unfortunately, all too easy to curtail or even drop the debriefing altogether. 'They were so involved that I didn't want to stop them' should be a challenge, not an excuse. Debriefings are very important. If you allow the event to over-run, then you should arrange for an adequate debriefing to be held the following day or the following week.

The Briefing

During the briefing make sure that you have your own checklist of things to say. Do not say too much. Do not give helpful hints in the area of policy. The participants are in charge of the action and, if they get it wrong, it will be an opportunity for experiential learning. Confine yourself to explaining the mechanics of the event – the timing, role allocation and resources. Ask for suggestions. But beware of overloading the event with technological resources – tape recorders, videocameras and the like – unless they are plausible within the scenario. There is also the risk of such hardware failing to work smoothly or quickly, thereby distracting your attention from the participants' behaviour.

The Action

Inherent in the concept of games and simulations is that power lies with the participants. During the action, a facilitator's task is simply to facilitate, not to train, teach or guide. One of the strengths of the methodology is that it confers authority on the participants. It is an affirmation of their importance in the learning process.

The proviso, of course, is that the participants must stay within the roles and rules. Players in a game must play to win, otherwise they are not competing and competition is the unwritten rule. Participants in a simulation must also accept their roles. They must not become wreckers. They must not play the clown. Doing so would reduce the simulation to sabotage.

The aim of the methodology is experiential learning. The participants must be allowed to make their own mistakes. For the facilitator to try to train, teach, instruct or guide would be to misconceive the basis of the methodology. When running the events try to be invisible. Answer questions about the mechanics ('Can we use the spare room?') but if asked a question of policy ('Should we elect a leader?') then reply that you are not present. This invisible cloak puts you in a favourable position to observe what is going on.

Intervene only in the case of sabotage or of a misunderstanding so great that it threatens to ruin the event.

The Debriefing

Although emotions are likely to be the focal point in the debriefing do not worry if you know little about psychology, psychotherapy, transactional analysis or other methodologies of the mind. The aim is not to psychoanalyse but to raise participants' awareness about their own and others' emotions. However, beware of turning the debriefing into an inquisition, particularly into the emotions of individuals. Respect personal privacy. People should not fear embarrassment.

Do not be dismayed if the debriefing ends with no clear-cut explanations. In any good game or simulation the participants will debrief themselves in the hours and days following the event. Such retrospective learning and awareness is particularly valuable because it occurs in private and without pressure. Remember, the first aim in the debriefing is to look at what happened.

Wherever possible, opt for a preliminary mini-debriefing in groups or pairs. One technique is to supply clipboards and a questionnaire and ask the participants to move around the whole group and interview each other. The findings from these preliminary soundings can then be reported to the whole group for comment, explanation and discussion.

It is common practice, though not obligatory, for the facilitator to chair the debriefing. If you have one or two assistant facilitators then consider allowing them to run the debriefing, but discuss this with them a day or two before the event to give them time to prepare. This is consistent with the philosophy of conferring power, and you can still have the last word.

Introduction

Assessment

Assessment is inevitable. If it is not done in public then it will occur in private. You will be assessed, as well as the participants. Assessment is a recurring aspect of human nature; it is part of learning by experience.

Formal assessment takes place when it is desirable to diagnose, understand, compare, select and evaluate on an official level – for example, when a game or simulation is run as an aid to recruitment or selection.

Whether the assessment is formal or informal and is carried out in private or in public, the basis is categorization. This book helps expand the categories to include the emotional aspects which are often excluded in traditional assessments of skills, knowledge and intelligence.

There is no special difficulty about categorizing the emotional side of behaviour. We all know what it is like to feel satisfaction, anger, fear and friendliness. The aim is not to measure these emotional responses – no machine can do that – but to be aware of the nature of the emotions and take them into account in an assessment.

Three Favourites

My three favourites among this collection of games and simulations are Planet Zita, Newsroom and Double Leap. All are easy to understand and run, simple in structure and yet challenging in practice. All are improved versions of some of my early ideas, and all three are highly involving. Run any of them and the emotions involved will be clearly evident.

PLANET ZITA

The emotions involved in Planet Zita relate to a life-or-death situation. The space crew have 21 days in which to find Base Area and they must find moisture and essential minerals on the way. Each of the five members of the space crew has important information (given in the Knowledge Cards). Crew member Andover has produced a map square showing the area where they landed. Crew member Dewsbury has a 21-day diary. Each day they can travel north, south, east or west and, when they have decided which way to go, another map square is provided which shows that area.

No one can save themselves; it has to be all or nothing. No one can opt out, no one can leave the others in the lurch – all have to contribute. They have to share their knowledge and share their ideas or the space crew dies. It is not easy for them. Survival depends on one or two common-sense ideas, such as not going beyond the point of no return. At first, it may seem to the participants that it is a matter of luck whether or not they can get to Base Area, but this is not so.

As mentioned earlier, this is a simulation you can try out on your own or preferably with family, friends or colleagues. See if the group can reach Base Area.

NEWSROOM

We all see or hear so many news bulletins that it must be easy to compile one – or is it? One difficulty, as mentioned in the Alpha Television Guidance for Candidates, is that the deadline is immutable. The bulletin must be ready on time. There is no possibility of pleading 'Please give us another minute, we're not quite ready.'

Another problem is that writing for radio or television is different from writing books, articles or letters. If something we read is not clear, the eye can turn back, but the ear does not have this facility. So things must be explained as one goes along. When using the spoken word it is important to start with who is speaking and go on to what is said, not vice versa. So the task is not simply to select the news items but to rewrite them if necessary.

Like Planet Zita the structure of Newsroom is cooperative. The journalists must cooperate, explain and inform. There is no winner – everyone is in the same boat. If an important story comes in – say, a train crash – and the person who receives it pushes it to one side and says nothing, then the journalists are in trouble.

The emotions concern news and time, and if the journalists don't work efficiently they will find that there is too much news and too little time. But, in practice, the participants thoroughly enjoy the situation, take pride in what they have done and end up with feelings of elation.

You can assess the event on your own – look at one story after another and see which stories you would have accepted, rejected or rewritten.

DOUBLE LEAP

Teams have to construct a slope for two marbles and include at least one leap through the air. The only construction materials are A4 paper and glue.

Compared with routine construction exercises ('Build the highest tower that you can') Double Leap has a plausible background and calls for artistry and imagination. The constructions must have a storyline – what do the two marbles represent? Events which involve both construction and imagination usually achieve a high profile. Outsiders hear of it and become interested.

With Double Leap the participants tend to produce a variety of construction features. There are straight slopes, curves, corkscrew shapes, loop-the-loop and leaping into funnels. The storylines also vary considerably – a cops and robbers chase, escaping from the volcano, Alice running after the White Rabbit, an attack by alien spaceships and so on.

Points are awarded for safety, elegance of design, excitement, the storyline, the cooperative effort involved and the presentation afterwards.

If adequate time is allowed for the construction and the development of the storyline, the results are likely to be highly rewarding and emotionally satisfying for all concerned.

As with Newsroom and Planet Zita, the emotions in Double Leap relate to fellow-feelings, togetherness, support, sympathy and enjoyment – including the enjoyment of the facilitator.

Emotional Word List

Some answers to the question 'How do you feel?'

acquiescent
affectionate
aggressive
alarmed
amazed
amused
angry
animosity
annoyed
anxious
apathetic
apprehensive
ardent
awestruck
benevolent
bewildered
bitter
blissful
bored
brave
caring
cautious
cheerful
competent
competitive
confident
contemptuous
contented
cool
cordial
cowardly
cross
curious
defeated
defensive
dejected
delighted
depressed
devoted
disappointed
discontented

discouraged
disgusted
disheartened
dismayed
dispassionate
disrespectful
distrustful
docile
eager
earnest
elated
enjoyment
enthusiastic
envious
excited
expectant
fair
faithful
fascinated
fearful
forceful
forgiving
fractious
frantic
friendly
frivolous
furious
gentle
grateful
greedy
happy
hatred
hopeful
hopeless
hostile
humble
humorous
hysterical
impassive
impatient
impulsive

indifferent
inspired
interested
intolerant
irritated
jealous
joyful
kind
lazy
lighthearted
loving
meek
melancholic
nervous
obedient
optimistic
passionate
passive
pathetic
patient
peaceful
pessimistic
philosophical
pitiful
pleasant
pleased
poetical
pompous
proud
provocative
rapturous
reckless
regretful
relieved
reluctant
remorseful
repulsed
resentful
resilient
respectful
responsive

restful
restrained
revolted
ridiculous
righteous
romantic
sad
satisfied
sensitive
serene
shamed
shocked
shy
sincere
smug
spiteful
stimulated
stoical
stressful
stubborn
sulky
surprised
suspicious
sympathetic
tense
tolerant
tranquil
triumphant
trusting
uncaring
uncertain
understanding
unfair
unkind
unpleasant
unworried
upset
vain
vehement
warm
worried

Facilitator's Checklist

Start with your own emotions. These are extremely important. Go through the Emotional Word List and select three or four that match your feelings.

If you select such words as 'enthusiastic' and 'confident' you are probably experienced and know what to do and how to do it. Even so, it is worthwhile looking at the following suggestions to see if a somewhat different approach is worth trying. If your selected words include 'worried' or 'apprehensive' then you should seek reassurance by involving colleagues and/or some of the participants themselves.

1. Before running a game or simulation consider appointing one or two participants to help brief, run and debrief the event. You could ask for volunteers, choose randomly or make your own selection. The co-opted participants can probably anticipate their colleagues' reactions better than you can. Show them the materials including the Emotional Word List and this Checklist. You may be surprised by their helpful suggestions. Delegating authority gives you a better opportunity to monitor what occurs.
2. During the briefing make sure that you have your own checklist of things to say. Do not say too much. Do not give helpful hints in the area of policy. The participants are in charge of the action and, if they get it wrong, it will be an opportunity for experiential learning. Confine yourself to explaining the mechanics of the event – the timing, role allocation and resources.
3. When running the event try to be invisible.
4. Wherever possible, opt for a preliminary mini-debriefing in groups or pairs. If you have one or two assistant facilitators, then consider allowing them to run the debriefing but discuss this with them a day or two before the event to give them time to prepare.
5. One technique for eliciting individual ideas in a debriefing is to give each participant a clipboard and questionnaire and ask them to interview each other in pairs.

Emotional Games: Summary

Title	Description	Notes	Running time
Playing Games	A simulation involving Trainees and Tutors at the Central Training College in the Republic of Alpha. The Trainees make presentations to the Tutors to explain the nature of games.	Planning and delivering a presentation is an emotional experience; particularly when the subject matter is so open-ended. Working as a team with others can generate both positive and negative emotions when there is pressure to perform.	60 to 120 minutes
About Face	A simulation about international traders from six countries. Each trader tries to acquire four units of the same sort of goods – food, clothes, books or tools. Unbeknown to the participants, each trader's name has an unfavourable association in the language of one of the other traders.	Negotiations often involve a whole range of emotions – some positive and some negative. In this case, each trader faces the delicate question of whether or not to reveal knowledge about the name of one of the other traders.	60 to 120 minutes depending on group size
Double Leap	A simulation about the construction of a slope made out of paper and glue, down which two marbles run and leap into space. The construction must be given a storyline. It is a test for applicants seeking a job at Alpha Structures.	Some people thrive on competition. But while there are positive emotions associated with winning, there are also the losers to consider. The creativity and the manual dexterity demanded from this exercise can also be sources of both positive and negative emotion.	60 minutes to a half-day, depending on group size and application
Leisure	It is 2000 years ago. Smoke appearing on Far Distant Mountain has thrown the local tribe into panic. What does the smoke portend? What action shall they take? Four proposals have been put forward for discussion at the tribal gathering.	Responding to perceived external challenge is a source of mixed emotion for many people in organizations. The process of communicating and agreeing a course of action is fraught with issues of peer judgement, group loyalty, fear of failure and potential conflict.	60 minutes. Longer with larger groups
Planet Zita	Planet Zita involves a test at the Central Business School in the Republic of Alpha. Groups of five students take part in an event in which each group is the crew of a spaceship, which has crashed on the planet Zita, struggling for their survival.	Win or lose situations in business generate extremes of emotion – euphoria at success and anxiety, anger and disgust at setback or failure. The team in which you work can be a source of inspiration and support or of irritation and frustration.	30 to 60 minutes

Emotional Games: Summary

Title	Description	Notes	Running time
Interest	This is a game about the creation of groups and access to groups. Players meet in pairs and can, if they wish, set up an 'interest group' with its own password. Players may also recruit other players into already-formed interest groups.	Inclusion and exclusion in groups or teams is a major source of positive and negative emotions at work. Loyalty to a particular group can generate noble emotions and behaviour towards our co-members and the basest emotions and behaviours towards those outside the group.	30 to 90 minutes
Newsroom	Alpha Television is recruiting journalists from newspapers to work in the Television News Department. As part of the selection procedure the applicants take part in the simulation of a news broadcast.	Time pressure and an unfamiliar role or task may be familiar issues at work and they generate a variety of emotions. Limited freedom of action, externally imposed rules and competition will almost always heighten the emotions we experience.	60 to 90 minutes
Happiness Project	The executives of four departments of PsychoSciences Inc. in the Republic of Alpha are asked to come up with ideas following the complete failure of Professor Pringle's Joy Monitor to measure happiness.	There's nothing like the threat of changing circumstances for exposing emotions associated with success or failure; self-interest or corporate interest; support or blame.	60 minutes Longer with larger groups
Secrecy	Alpha Allstate Insurance Company Inc. in the Republic of Alpha is holding a series of meetings in one of its hospitality suites to discuss ways of preventing computer fraud. Unbeknown to the company, the Security Manager has committed fraud and is using interviews with experts to try and find the information that would help cover up the crime.	Fraud is often a crime about which people may be ambivalent. How we react to fraud, secrecy and duplicity can be a source of many conflicting emotions and behaviours.	60 to 120 minutes
Creating Events	Creative Activities Inc. in the Republic of Alpha is running a selection procedure for people applying for jobs in the Editorial Department. The applicants try to devise a game or simulation relating to business ethics (or lack of ethics) and then present their ideas in a creative way.	Both the process and the content of Creating Events are sources for exploring what we believe and feel. The process of generating ideas and preparing a presentation can be fulfilling and fun, as well as threatening and worrying. The content allows people to express and demonstrate their perception of ethics.	60 to 120 minutes, depending on group size
Feeling Virtuous	This is a game in which the object is to make the most accurate guess about the ranking order of the virtues chosen by all the participants. The virtues are justice, truth, beauty, humour, faith, hope and charity.	Only the most self-aware are conscious of all of the beliefs that influence how they feel and behave at work. Exploring the virtues allows people to explore their personal values and provides them with an insight into how their colleagues think and feel too.	60 minutes Longer with larger groups

Emotional Games: Summary

Title	Description	Notes	Running time
Boat Tax	The time is hundreds of years ago. A tribe has introduced currency to replace barter. The highest piece of currency is a blue stone. The tribe levies a monthly tax of one blue stone on every working person and a yearly tax of two blue stones on the use of boats more than four paces in length. A meeting of the tribe has been called by protesters on the grounds that the boat tax is unfair to the fishcatchers.	Organizations are made up of a variety of interest groups. Belonging to one or other group and the self-interest associated with that group generates diverse emotions. Notions of protest and natural justice may be common to us all, whatever our own local interests. Practical or financially attractive solutions to problems within organizations can be tempered by vested interest.	60 minutes. Longer with larger groups
Hunting Pink	A simulation set in the offices of South Alpha Culture involving the design of an event called Hunting Pink in which there are three groups – huntsmen, huntswomen and foxes. The foxes may also hunt and win if they outnumber the hunters. Huntsmen can hunt huntswomen and vice versa.	Deeply held beliefs or values generate strong emotions. No issues are more potentially inflammatory at work or in society at large than those of gender roles, violence against animals and elitism or discrimination. Allowing the participants to change the 'rules', and consequently the bases for their beliefs, offers a very valuable lesson on why we believe the things we do.	60 to 120 minutes depending on group size
Elite	The first two international exchange students from the Republic of Omega are due to arrive at the Central Training College in the Republic of Alpha. Both are from a racial group called Elits and, in Omega, it is taken for granted that their average intelligence is higher than the average of the rest of the population.	Our beliefs about human rights, intelligence and race define much of our behaviour at home or at work. Experiencing how to discuss emotive issues (of all kinds) at work is an essential lesson for all.	120 minutes
Way Out	An advertising agency – Alpha Promotions Inc. – has invited university graduates to apply for jobs in its Editorial Department. Part of the selection procedure comprises a test to invent and promote a fictional product that could be described as 'way out'.	Extreme ideas are liberating for some, while the pressure to generate them can be unwelcome for others. Cooperation and competition are two sides of the same coin for many of us at work. How we feel about each of them will define how we manage our various business relationships and how successful they are.	60 to 120 minutes depending on group size

The Games and Simulations

1 Playing Games

Facilitator's Notes

DESCRIPTION

A simulation involving Trainees and Tutors at the Central Training College in the Republic of Alpha. The Trainees make presentations to the Tutors to explain the nature of games.

AIMS

To reveal and explore the sort of emotions associated with:

- creating, planning, organizing and judging presentations
- working in a team
- speaking in public.

COMMENTS

This simulation is easy to run since most of the facilitator's work is undertaken by the participants in the role of Tutors. The debriefing is relatively easy because teams, including the team of Tutors, can debrief themselves and report back to the main group.

Playing Games has been chosen as the first simulation in this book partly because it deals with basic terminology – what does the word 'game' mean in relation to such activities as role-plays, simulations, exercises and drama?

TIME AND NUMBERS

Depending on the number of participants, allow between one and two hours. There should be at least two participants in each team, including the team of Tutors. The minimum number required to run this simulation is six – three teams of two, including a team of Tutors. There is no maximum number (the Identity Cards allow for up to six teams).

The room(s) should be so arranged as to permit team planning in relative privacy. There should also be an area for the Tutors to make their announcements, and the same area can probably be used for the presentations – with chairs arranged so that other participants can watch.

MATERIALS

- Notes for Participants – one for each participant

- Central Training College Test Sheet – one for each participant
- Definition Sheet – one card for each team
- Instructions for Tutors – one for each participant in the role of Tutor
- Identity Cards – one for each participant
- Resources for presentations – overhead projectors, flipcharts, coloured pens and so on

BRIEFING

Before the event, photocopy the material for participants and cut out the Identity Cards.

Hand out the Notes for Participants.

Discuss the mechanics of the event – the timing, the location of the teams and the resources (overhead projectors, flipcharts, and so on) that would be available if required.

Retrieve the Notes for Participants as this is not a document included in the action.

Remove clutter or any materials that are not associated with the event in order to enhance plausibility.

The Identity Cards provide names of colours for six teams. With fewer teams, discard the extra cards. Place the Identity Cards face down, ask the participants to select one each and then form into their appropriate groups of Trainees and Tutors.

Hand out the Test Sheet – one for each participant, including the Tutors. Give each Tutor a copy of the Instructions for Tutors and give each team of Trainees a Definition Sheet.

ACTION

Consult with the Tutors about the mechanics of the event – particularly about the order and timing of the presentations. Explain that they should answer questions only about the mechanics of the event. If they (or you) are asked about matters within the competence of the team – for example, 'Is it a good idea to elect a team leader?' or 'Are we allowed to take notes?' – they (and you) must decline to answer.

If the event spans two sessions, a suitable time for a break would be before the start of the presentations.

DEBRIEFING

Since the action will differ widely from team to team, it is recommended to start with each team (including the Tutors) debriefing themselves on their decisions and emotions and then reporting back to the main group so that a broad picture is available for discussion.

In both the mini-debriefings and the main debriefing use can be made of the Emotional Word List containing 164 words that could answer the question 'How do you feel?', particularly in relation to planning, play-acting and presenting.

In the field of games and simulations for education and training there is a good deal of controversy about definitions. There are two opposing views. One is to categorize by things (rules, tokens, and so on) and the other is to categorize by the motives of the participants within the event.

It is notoriously difficult to classify by things. To say, for example, that a game is a contest with rules would mean that all court cases, duels and musical competitions are games.

Since this book is about emotions it is appropriate to categorize by motives. Why are they doing what they are doing? Are they trying to win within the magic kingdom of a game or are they trying to behave professionally, taking account of the concerns and ethics of the real world?

As an example, consider two events dealing with property development. In a game, such as *Monopoly*, the participants are in the role of players. They have a duty to try to win. If they knock down houses in order to build hotels this is not unethical within the context of the game. However, in a property development simulation it could be regarded as unethical to knock down houses and there could be action from protest groups, officials and the media. In a simulation it is the environment that is simulated; the motives and emotions are real.

Using motives as the criteria for distinguishing games from simulations has several advantages. One is that it is immediately seen to be relevant in a business context. Another is that it helps trainers, facilitators and designers achieve a consistent methodology. It avoids mish-mash events in which some participants are trying to win a game whereas others are behaving professionally, and the very real possibility of damaging real-life personal relationships. The clash of methodologies is usually assumed to be due to a clash of personalities with the participants blaming each other and the facilitator blaming the participants.

Mish-mash events are not uncommon, so it is useful to bear in mind the question 'Why did you do what you did?'

When defined by the motives of the participants, games and simulations are not only completely different, they are incompatible. In order to avoid confusion it is best to avoid such terms as 'simulation-game'. It is better to say 'simulation or game'.

Consistency of methodology is important in order to avoid the unpleasantness that often results from incompatible methodologies.

Playing Games: Notes for Participants

This is a simulation involving Tutors and Trainees at the Central Training College – the national college for training trainers in the Republic of Alpha.

The event concerns a test of communication skills. Groups of Trainees make presentations about the way they define the word 'game', and these presentations must include at least one piece of drama. The Tutors have the task of organizing the timing of the presentations and assessing them.

Trainees can consult the Tutors if they want special facilities for their presentations but, if such facilities are not readily available, the Trainees can pretend that they exist.

At the end of the presentations the Tutors will comment briefly on each team's efforts but there will be no public announcement about individuals. It is College policy to conduct the assessment of individuals privately.

The procedures are explained in the Test Sheet for Trainees and the Instruction Sheet for the Tutors.

ALPHA CENTRAL TRAINING COLLEGE
Test Sheet for Trainees

This is a test in which our Tutors will assess your communication skills. Your task is to make a presentation to the Tutors (and the other teams) about the way you define the word 'game'. Your presentation must contain at least one playlet to show what is (and perhaps what is not) a game, according to your definition.

You can assume that the members of the audience are not involved in training and that they think games are (a) sports and (b) things sold in game shops.

Since the aim is to assess communication skills, you will lose marks if your team contains silent members, or members who say very little and say it hurriedly. The Tutors will help you with the mechanics of your presentation – the location, timing and any resources required, such as flipcharts.

Fill in your Definition Sheet and hand this to the Tutors before your presentation. The Tutors will introduce your team and will ask for questions from the audience after each presentation. Finally, they will probably give their general impressions of the presentations but will not comment on individuals.

Although all team members should speak during the presentation, the playlet(s) need not have any dialogue. For example, last year one team of four Trainees told the audience that they defined a game as a contest. They produced two playlets. Two Trainees sat at a chessboard while the other two Trainees explained that this demonstrated a contest in which the stronger player was trying to win and the weaker player was trying to draw. It was a game because it was a contest. The Trainees giving the explanations then changed places and sat at the chessboard. This was explained as being a television play in which two actors played rehearsed moves. It was play-acting, and therefore it was neither a contest nor a game.

Finally, please note that all team planning and discussion must cease once the presentations have started. You will lose marks if you try to continue the discussions. The audience should watch in respectful silence.

Good luck!

ALPHA CENTRAL TRAINING COLLEGE
Definition Sheet

Name of team _____

We define a 'game' as:

ALPHA CENTRAL TRAINING COLLEGE
Instructions for Tutors

ASSESSING THE PRESENTATIONS

You are responsible for organizing the mechanics of the test – the location, resources, timing and order of the presentations. Find adequate areas for the team planning stage and allocate a space (stage) for the presentations.

You may find it a good idea to give one Tutor the responsibility of making sure that teams do not over-run the time allowed for their presentations.

You should not give them any advice on the contents of their presentation.

Your job entails:

1. introducing each team – 'This is the green team and their definition is ...'
2. thanking each team afterwards and calling for questions
3. closing the event with a few remarks in general terms. Avoid criticizing any individuals – individual assessments are done in committee at the end of the week.

Work as a team and take it in turns to introduce the teams and make comments.

Identity Cards – cut out

Red Team

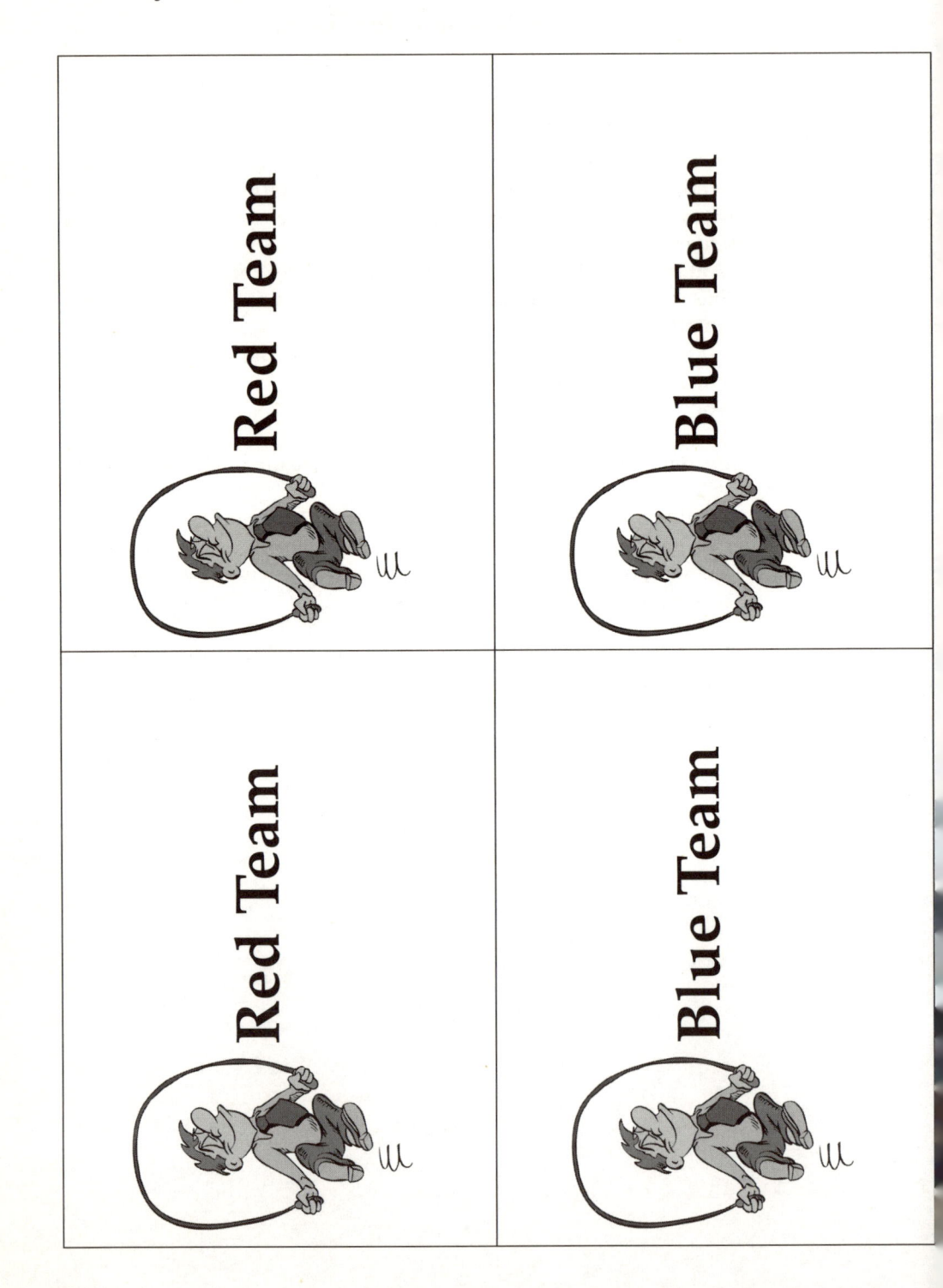

Blue Team

Red Team

Blue Team

© Ken Jones, *Emotional Games for Training*, Gower Publishing Limited, 2002

Identity Cards – continued

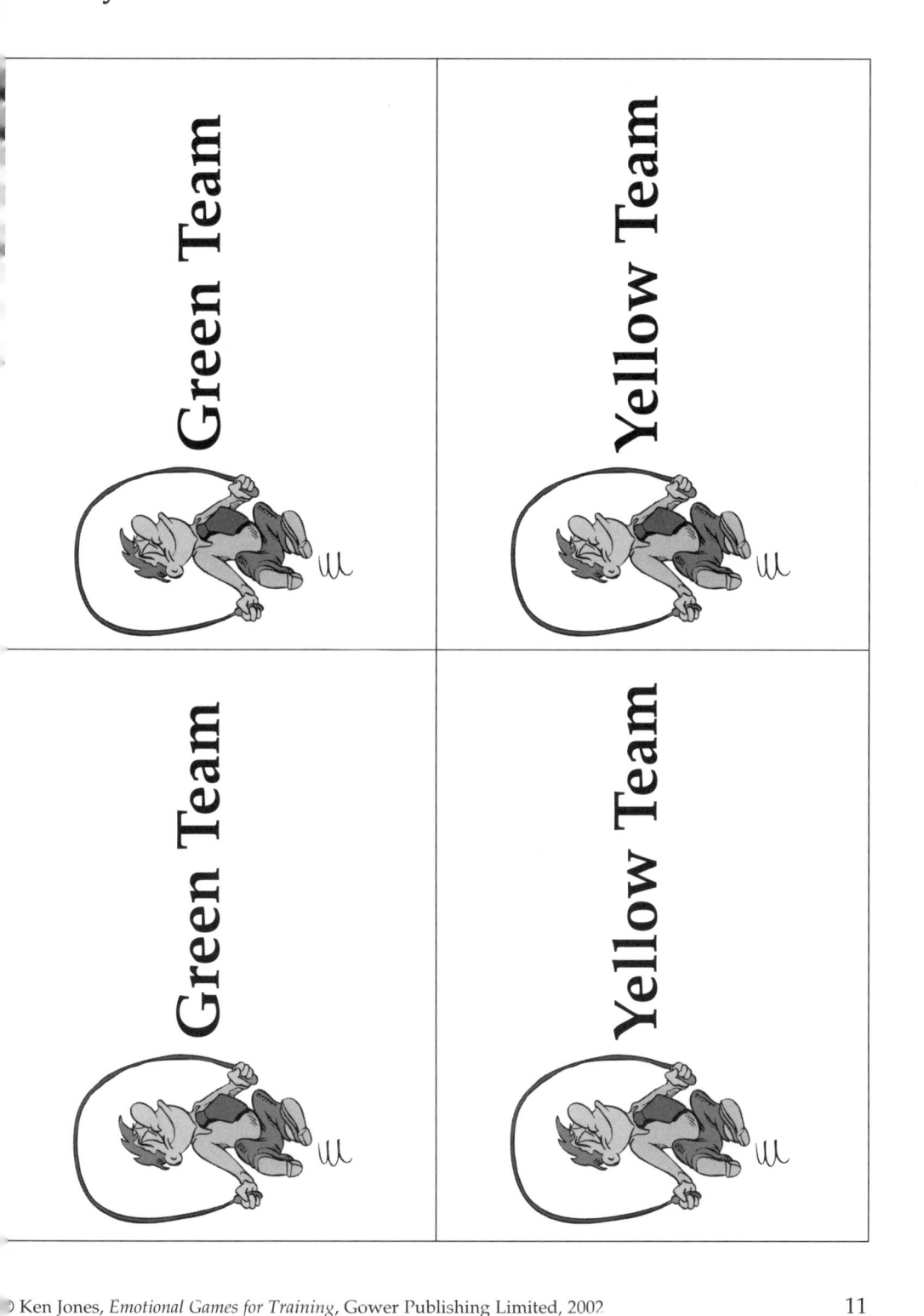

| Green Team | Yellow Team |
| Green Team | Yellow Team |

Identity Cards – continued

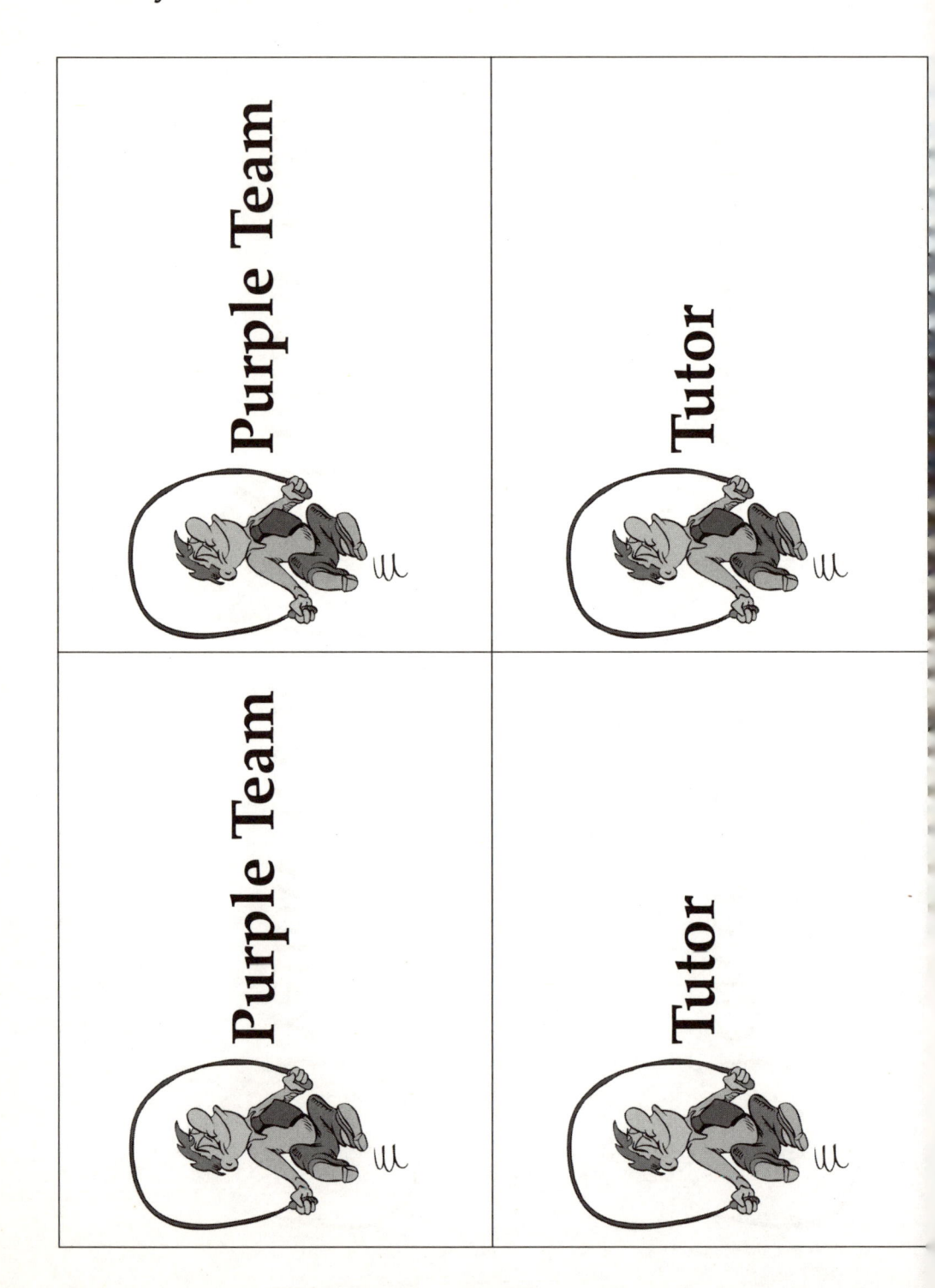

Purple Team	Tutor
Purple Team	Tutor

2 About Face

Facilitator's Notes

DESCRIPTION

A simulation about international traders from six different countries. Each trader tries to acquire four units of the same sort of goods – food, clothes, books or tools.

There is a hidden agenda – the name of each of the six traders is a word which has unfortunate associations in one of the other five languages.

With more than six participants, participants with the same name and same country work together with one set of Trading Cards, one International Trading Sheet and one Knowledge Card between them.

AIMS

To reveal the sort of emotions associated with negotiations and diplomacy, particularly the problem of whether to mention the unfortunate linguistic associations of a person's name.

COMMENTS

This simulation is easy to run because it can fit into a single period in which everyone is doing the same thing – trying to acquire four units of the same sort of goods.

It involves ethical decisions – whether to pass on the linguistic knowledge to anyone else, particularly to the person concerned.

It could be useful to recruit an assistant facilitator to help in handing out the cards and arranging the trading floor – decisions need to be made, for example, whether chairs and tables should be available and whether a clock should be prominent to help countries time their meetings. In addition, an assistant facilitator can answer queries and help make sure that each of the confidential Knowledge Cards is handed out to the traders from the appropriate country.

TIME AND NUMBERS

The minimum number for this event is six participants, in which case an hour should be allowed. If you have more than six participants allow up to two hours. You could take a break before the debriefing.

MATERIALS

- Notes for Participants – one for each participant
- Omega Rules of Trading – one for each country
- Omega International Trading Sheet – one for each country
- Six Identity Cards – one card for each participant
- Six (confidential) Knowledge Cards – one each for the appropriate country
- Trading Cards (food, clothes, books and tools) – a set for each of the six countries

BRIEFING

Before the event, photocopy the material for participants and cut out the required number of Identity, Knowledge and Trading Cards.

Hand out the Notes for Participants.

Discuss the mechanics of the event – space, trading area and timing – but take care not to reveal the nature of the Knowledge Cards.

Retrieve the Notes for Participants as this is not a document included in the action. Also make sure that the trading area is free of non-simulation clutter – textbooks, coats and so on.

Place the Identity Cards face down and allow the participants to choose their own. If there are more than six participants, ask those with the same name (and country) to form into groups. Hand out the six Knowledge Cards to the appropriate countries, making sure that they are not seen by the other countries.

Hand out to each country one copy of the Omega Rules of Trading, one copy of the Omega International Trading Sheet and one set of Trading Cards – one card each of food, clothes, books and tools.

ACTION

The simulation will probably run itself. However, if a country completes its trading by obtaining four of the same type of goods while the others are still struggling you could ask them to become observers or begin to discuss what they will say in the debriefing.

DEBRIEFING

This could begin with each country (in alphabetical order) disclosing what was written on the Knowledge Card. (Note that the Knowledge Cards are arranged so that, at any meeting, only one trader could have information about the name of the trader from the other country.)

The discussion can cover the emotions involved, particularly in relation to one's feelings about imparting bad news – 'In our country your name means ...'

Use the Emotional Word List (or your own selection of words) as a tool to help participants classify what they felt.

It may be useful for the participants to take it in turns to reveal their emotions. Did they feel guilty (uncomfortable, concerned, worried, amused, pleased) on reading the linguistic information? How did they feel if they (a) passed on the information to the trader with that name, (b) told other traders or (c) did not reveal the information?

When everyone has explained (briefly) what emotions they felt, you can lead the discussion down whatever avenue seems appropriate. This may include questions relating to emotions involved in communication skills, diplomacy and negotiations.

About Face: Notes for Participants

This is a simulation about international traders trying to acquire four units of the same sort of goods – food, clothes, books or tools.

You will be a trader from one of six countries – Alpha, Beta, Gamma, Delta, Epsilon and Zeta. You are employed by your country's National Trading Organization. The location is the International Trade Fair in the Republic of Omega.

If there are more than six participants you may find yourself in partnership with someone of the same name and from the same country. In this case, you must work together as a trading group and must not split up.

Each country receives a complete set of cards of the four types of goods, as well as a confidential Knowledge Card about aspects of the language of your country. Do not show this card to traders from other countries, although you may discuss the contents of the card if you so wish.

AIMS OF TRADE

There is no point-scoring as such, but at the end of the session there is more merit if you have acquired two units that are the same type of goods than if you still have all four types of goods. Two pairs of goods are better than one pair, and three of a kind are better than two pairs. Four units of the same goods have the highest merit.

Omega International Trade Fair

Rules of Trading

- All trading must be bilateral – three or more countries are not allowed to meet together.
- All trade is by barter on a one-for-one basis (all countries must always have four units) and credit is not allowed.
- Traders must record details of their meetings on the International Trading Sheet, even if no agreements are reached.
- There is no obligation for traders to disclose what units they hold, apart from the unit(s) they offer for exchange.
- In the interests of international understanding, friendship and respect, traders should aim to meet the representatives of all the other five countries and should time their meetings accordingly.
- Once traders have met representatives of the other five countries they can have more meetings for further trading or for social discussions, but only on a bilateral basis.

Omega International Trade Fair

International Trading Sheet

Name _____   Country _____

Name and country of foreign trader _____
I gave _____ in exchange for _____
Comments

Name and country of foreign trader _____
I gave _____ in exchange for _____
Comments

Name and country of foreign trader _____
I gave _____ in exchange for _____
Comments

Name and country of foreign trader _____
I gave _____ in exchange for _____
Comments

Name and country of foreign trader _____
I gave _____ in exchange for _____
Comments

Identity Cards – cut out

Anthod Republic of Alpha	**Bidil** Republic of Beta
Gamta Republic of Gamma	**Deffon** Republic of Delta
Epow Republic of Epsilon	**Zettel** Republic of Zeta

© Ken Jones, *Emotional Games for Training*, Gower Publishing Limited, 2002

Knowledge Cards – cut out

Anthod's knowledge

My country is the Republic of Alpha.

In Alphan language a 'bidil' is an evil spirit, usually, but not always, associated with bogs and marshes. There is a well-known nursery rhyme about the bidil's curse in which the bidil curses a young princess.

The phrase 'He's a bidil' means 'He's mean, unpleasant and unkind.'

Bidil's knowledge

My country is the Republic of Beta.

In Betan language the word 'gamta' means toxic waste – either nuclear waste or chemical waste. There has recently been a series of prosecutions of people who have dumped gamta illegally causing others to be contaminated.

The word is sometimes used in isolation – 'Gamta!' – as an expression of extreme annoyance or distaste.

Gamta's knowledge

My country is the Republic of Gamma.

In Gamman language the word 'deffon' refers to a type of criminal fraud – usually of a business nature – such as issuing a false prospectus or writing out a fraudulent cheque.

The phrase 'That's deffon' means 'That's cheating.'

Deffon's knowledge

My country is the Republic of Delta.

In Deltan language the word 'epow' means food which is unfit for human consumption. Recently several shopkeepers have been prosecuted for trying to sell epow to the public by disguising it with strong spices.

The phrase 'That's epow' means 'That's rubbish' or 'That's deceitful rubbish.'

© Ken Jones, *Emotional Games for Training*, Gower Publishing Limited, 2002

Knowledge Cards – continued

Epow's knowledge

My country is the Republic of Epsilon.

In the Epsilon language the word 'zettel' means treachery. In the fourteenth century Lord and Lady Zettel murdered the king by poisoning his food while pretending to be loyal subjects.

The phrase 'You're a zettel' means 'You're treacherous.' There is an Epsilon saying 'As deceitful as a zettel'.

Zettel's knowledge

My country is the Republic of Zeta.

In the Zetan language the word 'anthod' is a slang term for a prostitute, either male or female. It derives from the fourth-century cult of Anthod when Anthodians, both men and women, journeyed to towns to prostitute themselves for money.

To say 'You're an Anthod' is extremely insulting and means 'You've sold yourself.'

© Ken Jones, *Emotional Games for Training*, Gower Publishing Limited, 2002

Trading Cards – cut out

Clothes	Tools
Clothes	Tools

© Ken Jones, *Emotional Games for Training*, Gower Publishing Limited, 2002

Trading Cards – continued

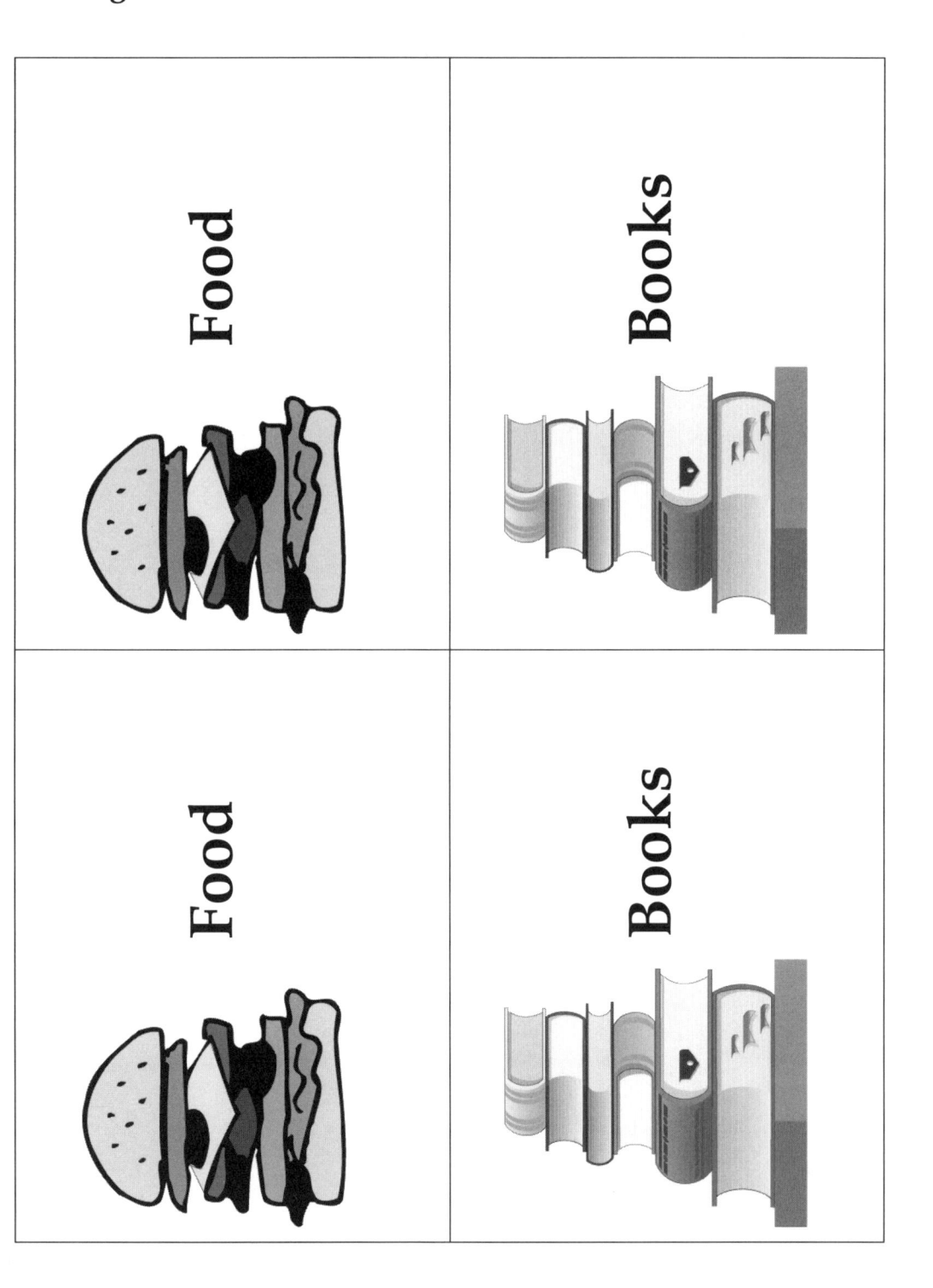

Food	Books
Food	Books

© Ken Jones, *Emotional Games for Training*, Gower Publishing Limited, 2002

3 Double Leap

Facilitator's Notes

DESCRIPTION

A simulation in which participants construct a slope made out of paper and glue down which two marbles run and leap through space. It is a test for applicants seeking a job at Alpha Structures.

AIMS

To reveal the sort of emotions associated with working with a fragile material in order to produce a sufficiently strong structure with exciting features and a creative storyline.

COMMENTS

This simulation is easy to run and could become a feature of a course. It is a good idea to include a break between the construction and the presentation phases.

TIME AND NUMBERS

The minimum number is nine participants – three teams of three. The minimum time is one hour. With larger numbers and more presentations, the event could last half a day or longer. You may prefer to allow participants to plan and construct in their own free time.

MATERIALS

- Notes for Participants – one for each participant
- Instructions for Applicants – one for each team
- Publicity Sheet – one for each team
- Executive's Score Sheet – one for each of the Executives
- Ten sheets of A4 plus two marbles, glue, scissors, ruler and coloured pens for each team

BRIEFING

Before the event photocopy all materials for participants.
    Hand out the Notes for Participants.
    Discuss the mechanics of the event, including the work areas for

each team. Steps may be taken to ensure privacy but, in practice, teams do not wish to copy features from other teams.

Before and during the briefing you could discuss who should have the role of Alpha Structures Executives who judge the constructions. Should it be yourself, a team of participants, colleagues, friends or someone else?

Retrieve the Notes for Participants and remove any personal clutter that is inappropriate to the setting of the simulation.

Divide the participants randomly into teams of between three and four.

Hand out to each team the Instructions for Applicants, the Publicity Sheet and the materials – ten A4 sheets, two marbles, glue, scissors, ruler and coloured pens.

ACTION

The simulation will probably run itself. If participants are playing the role of Alpha Structures Executives, discuss with them how to run the mechanics of the event – for example, how to order the presentations. You can suggest what facilities might be available if requested but, of course, leave the decision-making to them.

As suggested earlier, it is a good idea to have breaks so that the teams can consider and reconsider the construction and the presentation. Best results are achieved if the action is not crammed into one session. It could even be spread over periods and last for two or three days.

DEBRIEFING

This could begin with each team debriefing itself and then explaining to the others the emotions they felt during the processes of design, construction and presentation.

Of special interest are the feelings involved in creating something within a group – the interchange of ideas and the personality differences over issues of initiative and leadership.

The presentations offer enormous scope for teamwork, enjoyment and emotions – including the emotions of the audience. Does the team dress up in white coats? Do they sing a promotional song? Do they fill a flipchart with masses of (imaginary) equations?

When innovations occur it is always worthwhile exploring the accompanying emotions.

Double Leap: Notes for Participants

This is a simulation in which students who have passed their architectural examinations are seeking positions at the prestigious company of Alpha Structures.

As part of the assessment procedure they are divided into teams and given the task of constructing a slope made out of paper and glue down which two marbles run and leap through space. Each team is also asked to create a storyline – what does the journey of the marbles represent?

You are an applicant or, if there are sufficient numbers, you might be one of the company's Executives in charge of the test and assessment.

The company's requirements are explained in Instructions for Applicants. Another document – the Publicity Sheet – is to be used by each team to give itself a name, name the construction and write a few words about it that can be used in the presentation.

It is worth spending some time on the presentation. Who will say what? To what extent, if any, can the storyline be built into the structure itself?

ALPHA STRUCTURES
Instructions for Applicants

Congratulations on having had a successful interview and reaching the shortlist.

You are now invited to participate as teams in a test to assess your ability to contribute to the planning, construction and presentation of a structure made of not more than ten sheets of A4 paper and glue. No other materials are allowed. The structure must consist of a slope down which two marbles run and make at least one leap across space. At the top of the slope, the marbles must be touching each other and then be released either by hand or a release mechanism. At the bottom of the run, the marbles should slow down rather than crash.

You will be given a sufficient supply of glue and ten sheets of A4 paper. You are not allowed to glue the construction to any surface – if you wish it to have a base then it must be made from the sheets of paper.

In addition, you must devise a storyline to explain what is being represented. You will also have a Publicity Sheet on which you write the name of your team (you could use your real names or a fantasy name), the name of your structure, and a storyline. What do the structure and the marbles represent? (For example, it could represent a dog chasing a ball.) The Publicity Sheet should then be placed in front of your construction while you explain and demonstrate it to the other teams.

In particular, we shall be looking at your teamwork and your flair in terms of planning, construction and presentation. Up to ten points will be awarded for the following, making a possible total of 60 points:

Safety and stability. Points will be deducted if the marbles come off the track, if the construction collapses or if the marbles crash at the end of the run.

Elegance. Artistry of design is appreciated.

Excitement. Points will be lost if the structure is a dull, dead straight affair.

Storyline. We will be looking for evidence of imagination and will be interested in seeing how well the storyline is reflected in the structure.

Presentation. We will be hoping for flair and confidence.

Cooperation. We will not be impressed if we see that one or two members of the team are 'passengers' in the planning, construction and presentation.

Good luck to all teams!

ALPHA STRUCTURES
Publicity Sheet

Team name: _____

Name of construction: _____

Storyline:

ALPHA STRUCTURES
Executive's Score Sheet

	Teams				
Safety and stability					
Elegance					
Excitement					
Storyline					
Presentation					
Cooperation					
Total					

4 Leisure

Facilitator's Notes

DESCRIPTION

It is 2000 years ago. Smoke appearing on Far Distant Mountain has caused concern in the local tribe. Four proposals have been put forward for discussion at the tribal gathering. These proposals relate to strength, faith, the market and games.

AIMS

To reveal the sort of emotions that arise when:

- planning a case, presenting it and negotiating
- dealing with the unusual.

COMMENTS

This simulation is easy to run. The procedure of the tribal meeting is laid down in the Way of the Gathering – only the person holding the Talking Rod is allowed to speak.

The simulation tends to involve the participants in a way that is emotionally different from that of a management game.

TIME AND NUMBERS

The minimum number is ten – two participants for each group including the Impartials. In this case, the simulation will probably last for an hour, but allow longer if you have larger numbers.

MATERIALS

- Notes for Participants – one for each participant
- The Way of the Gathering – one copy for each group
- Plans for Leisure – one for each group
- Identity Cards – one for each participant
- Knowledge Cards – one card for each group
- One Talking Rod – perhaps a wooden ruler or even a bit of a branch

BRIEFING

Before the event, photocopy the materials for participants and cut out the required number of Knowledge and Identity Cards.

Hand out the Notes for Participants.

Discuss the mechanics of the simulation – the timing, the group areas, the area for the tribal meeting and possibly areas for breaks and private negotiations.

Retrieve the Notes for Participants and remove any non-tribal clutter from the area.

Place the Identity Cards face down and let the participants pick one each. They can then divide into their groups – Strength, Faith, Market, Games and Impartials.

Hand out to each group a copy of the Way of the Gathering, the Plans for Leisure and the appropriate Knowledge Card.

Give the Talking Rod to one of the Impartials.

ACTION

The tribal meeting procedures have a basic simplicity, and the discipline of the Way of the Gathering encourages the participants to have an orderly meeting. Depending on the time available, try to have at least one or two breaks in which the groups can negotiate privately.

You should reply to any questions with respect to the mechanics of the event – for example, 'Can we use the spare room?' – or refer the question to the Impartials. If asked questions of fact – say, 'How many members are in the tribe?' – then you can say that you don't know or that you are not a member of the tribe.

DEBRIEFING

It is a good idea to start with the groups debriefing themselves and then reporting back and revealing what was on their Knowledge Cards.

The emotions aroused in this simulation may depend on the extent to which individual participants put themselves in the role of a member of an ancient tribe. Did they feel the mystique of the Way of the Gathering? Did they try to respect the tribal traditions? Did their behaviour and language match the situation in which they found themselves?

Most or all of the participants will have probably felt the emotion of tribal loyalty. But also of interest are the emotions involved in dealing with the unusual.

Leisure: Notes for Participants

You are members of a tribe that lived 2000 years ago.

At the time of the last moon, smoke was seen on Far Distant Mountain. Yesterday evening it was seen again. No other tribe lives anywhere nearby and no member of the tribe has been to the Mountain.

Until recently, each individual made everything they needed – their own pots, huts, garments and arrows. Now there are garment-makers, potters, arrowsmiths and hutbuilders and the goods are exchanged. This new system has resulted in more and better goods and a saving in time. Consequently, now the tribe has more leisure time.

A 'Gathering of the Tribe' will be held to take decisions on the Plans for Leisure. All members sit in their own groups according to the plan they support – strength, faith, the market and games. The Impartials are in charge of the Gathering but do not have a vote. The procedure for the meeting is explained in the Way of the Gathering.

Another document contains the four plans, and each group has a Knowledge Card giving the basic position which it must put forward at the Gathering, but which can be modified (or abandoned) later.

The Way of the Gathering

The Talking Rod is the way of friendship, the way of love, the way of wisdom and the way of the tribe.

The person who holds the Talking Rod must speak and then pass the rod on round the Gathering. Those who do not hold the Talking Rod must listen to the words and stay silent.

The Impartials are in charge of the meeting, but no Impartial has a vote. An Impartial shall start the meeting by holding the Talking Rod and reading out the Plans.

The Impartials shall help the tribe talk about what it wants to discuss.

Plans for Leisure

STRENGTH PLAN

Our plan is to build a stockade, make weapons and train people to use weapons.

FAITH PLAN

Our plan is to build a house for the gods and for training the people who will become the Keepers of the Faith.

MARKET PLAN

Our plan is to build a good market with storehouses for keeping food and other goods.

GAMES PLAN

Our plan is for games and sports, dancing, music, poetry, storytelling and philosophy. Huts should be built for music and the arts.

Leisure

Identity Cards – cut out

💪	**Strength**	💪	**Strength**
🧘	**Faith**	🧘	**Faith**
🧺	**Market**	🧺	**Market**
🏃	**Games**	🏃	**Games**
⚖️	**Impartials**	⚖️	**Impartials**

Knowledge Cards – cut out

Strength group's knowledge

The smoke is a warning to us. We need strength. We need weapons and we need to know how to fight to protect our tribe.

We are not against games and markets but defence must come first.

We must speak to the Faith group. They believe in the strength of the tribe.

Faith group's knowledge

We need faith – faith now and faith in the future. We need faith in this life and faith in the next life. The gods are strong, the gods are just, the gods will nourish our spirits.

The Market group think of goods. The Strength group think of war. We think of the gods.

We must speak to the Games group. They believe in peace, beauty and truth.

Market group's knowledge

The market is the first thing. The market has made our lives better. The market is for each and for all, in which all are equal to make, buy and sell. It is not just a place, it is an idea – the idea of peace, progress and freedom.

We are not against games or faith, but the market is the rock that supports all else. And now we need protection. We should speak to the Strength group.

Knowledge Cards – continued

Games group's knowledge

In our leisure time we can play games, take part in sports, sing and dance, speak philosophy and poetry and tell the stories of our tribe. We can live in love.

We believe in equality and peace. We fear temples and priests; we fear armies and soldiers. We want peace in which each person is equal with another in freedom and joy.

We should speak to the Market group. They believe in equality and freedom.

Impartials' knowledge

We, the Impartials, are the servants of the tribe. We hold the knowledge of the law and it is our duty to serve the tribe in reason and in fairness.

If some members of the tribe think that something is unfair or unjust or wrong, then let a plan be put forward. It is not a matter for us; it is a matter for the tribe.

If some members of the tribe think that a plan should be changed or that the tribe should do something that it does not yet do, then let that matter be put forward. Let each speak as they feel. It is not a matter for us; it is a matter for the tribe. We help the tribe talk about what they want to talk about.

We can always voice our views, but we must not be unreasonable or unfair. We should speak together before we speak to the tribe. We are the Impartials.

5 Planet Zita

Facilitator's Notes

DESCRIPTION

Planet Zita involves a test at the Central Business School in the Republic of Alpha. Groups of five students take part in an event in which each group is the crew of a spaceship which has crashed on the planet Zita. Their task is to survive.

AIMS

To reveal the emotions associated with cooperation and leadership (or non-leadership) in a test scenario which simulates a life-or-death situation.

COMMENTS

This event generates considerable involvement and excitement. It is easy to understand, but it is difficult for the space crew to survive.

TIME AND NUMBERS

The ideal number of participants is five, or groups of five. If you wish, you may have one or more participants in the role of Tutor to organize the event and comment afterwards on the efforts of the team(s).
    Allow between half an hour and an hour for the whole event.

MATERIALS

- Notes for Participants – one copy for each participant
- Instructions and Hints about Planet Zita – one copy for each participant
- Five Knowledge Cards for Andover, Burnley, Cardiff, Dewsbury and Exeter
- Dewsbury's 21-Day Diary – one copy for Dewsbury
- Map Squares – one pack of 41 cards for each space crew

BRIEFING

Before the event, photocopy the materials for participants and cut out the Knowledge Cards. Cut out the Map Squares and arrange them in numerical order ready to hand out as requested by the crew(s).

Hand out the Notes for Participants and discuss the mechanics of the event – the location of the space crew(s) and the timing. If you have several groups, keep them as separate as possible. Use a large table or the floor for laying out the Map Squares.

Retrieve the Notes for Participants and remove any non-space-like clutter from the area.

Divide the participants randomly into groups of five and, if desired, have a few participants in the role of Tutors to supervise the event – mainly by handing out the Map Squares on request – and to comment afterwards.

Hand out the Instructions and Hints about Planet Zita – one to each participant. Place the five Knowledge Cards face down and let the participants pick their own. Give Dewsbury's 21-Day Diary to Dewsbury and give Map Square 1 to Andover, to be placed in the middle of the group.

Avoid giving any hints. In particular, do not say anything along the lines of 'You don't have to keep moving forward; you are allowed to retrace your steps.'

ACTION

Keep each pack of Map Squares separate on a table ready to be handed out on request – for example, 'We want to go north to the trees on Map Square 13.' A good way to avoid confusing one pack with another is to arrange the packs so that they are aligned with the layout of the tables or the position of the groups in the training room.

The simulation will run itself, leaving you well placed to observe what is going on.

If you have one or more participants as Tutors then you can discuss arrangements with them while the space crew are deciding which way to go on the first day. Impress on the Tutors that they must not give out any hints.

In the event of death it is for you (or the Tutors) to decide whether you should allow the crew to come back to life, hand back the fatal Map Squares and continue to try to find Base Area.

DEBRIEFING

Invite the space crews to start the process by holding their own mini-debriefing and handing round their Knowledge Cards. This will reveal whether all the vital pieces of information were passed on. (**Note**: each piece of vital information – leadership, ash, hills, sand, trees, brank, Base Area, days for survival – is contained on more than one Knowledge Card.)

Emotions will depend partly on whether the participants treated the test lightheartedly or seriously. How did the group react to survival or, more likely, death? Another emotional point concerns leadership. What were the emotions involved in picking, or not picking, a leader and what happened afterwards as a result of this decision?

Did an individual's actual gender play a part? Were males more aggressive or domineering perhaps? If so, what emotions were aroused?

RATIONALE

The crews will survive if they remember the following points:

- Never pass the point of no return – that is, never travel more than two days away from trees (moisture), except for the final days when they are within sight of Base Area.
- More information about the planet can be gained by going in a straight line than by turning left or right.
- On the first day it is best to go south to brank (vital minerals) and then return to the trees (moisture) in the north. To go to the trees first means that it is not possible to return to that particular patch of brank, and there is very little brank on Zita.

Planet Zita: Notes for Participants

This simulation involves a test at the Central Business School in the Republic of Alpha involving a spaceship that has gone adrift and landed on Planet Zita – a hostile planet.

The crew have to decide on the direction to travel across the planet to try to reach Base Area.

There is no map of the planet but you will receive a Map Square showing the area of the crash and what can be seen of the areas located one day's walk away to the north, south, east and west. Once the crew have decided which way to go, they will receive another Map Square showing that particular area and what can be seen further away. Each member of the crew – Andover, Burnley, Cardiff, Dewsbury and Exeter – will have their own Knowledge Card. In addition, Andover will have Map Square 1 and Dewsbury will have a 21-Day Diary.

The situation is explained in Instructions and Hints about Planet Zita.

CENTRAL BUSINESS SCHOOL

Instructions and Hints about Planet Zita

Welcome to Planet Zita. You have crashed, the planet is hostile and it is easy to die. Prior to the crash, you were adrift in space: no one knows where to look for you, so you must try to find Base Area.

You will each receive a Knowledge Card telling you what you know about Zita. Obviously, the cards do not really exist on Zita; they represent information in your heads, so you should not show your card to anyone else. However, if you want to make sure that you pass on the full and correct information you are allowed to read your card aloud to the others.

You do not have a map of Zita, but Andover has Map Square 1 showing where you landed and what you can see one day's walk away. Dewsbury has a 21-Day Diary.

The test is simple, but not easy. Decide which way to go and ask for that particular Map Square by its number.

Make sure that each day's movements are recorded in Dewsbury's Diary – do not just leave it to Dewsbury to remember to fill it in.

In order to avoid confusion about where you are, it is useful to use a coin to mark the square you are on.

You are not allowed to travel diagonally. Sorry, but there it is. You go either north, south, east or west each day. And you are not allowed to split up. You must all stick together.

If (or perhaps when) you die, you will be given the remainder of the pack of Map Squares and you should begin your own mini-debriefing. However, you can make a special request to be allowed to hand back the fatal Map Squares and continue. Afterwards, the Tutors may comment on each team's efforts.

On Planet Zita your emotions are important. Feeling impetuous is highly dangerous.

Knowledge Cards – cut out

Andover's knowledge

My name is Andover – Space Officer.

We have problems. Our spaceship lost radio contact and went adrift. We have landed on the planet Zita – a dangerous, volcanic planet.

Our radio cannot be repaired and no one is likely to look for us here. Our supplies of food and water were destroyed in the crash. Our captain is dead and, under Emergency Regulations, we can choose a leader if we wish to do so.

We must find the Base Area where Zitans live. It has a large radio mast and we should be able to see it two days' walk away. If we climbed a hill we could see further.

I have made a Map Square showing where we have landed and what we can see one day's walk away to the north, east, south and west. I have numbered it Map Square 1.

As we travel I will make other Map Squares to add to it, giving them random numbers.

At present, we are on grass. If we travel west to Map Square 18 there is more grass and one day's walk further on is a hill. If we go north – I have numbered the square 13 – we will arrive at an area of trees. If we go east – Map Square 5 – we will be in a sandy area. And if we go south to Map Square 24 there is a sort of shrub called brank which has vital minerals.

I have heard that walking on ash may be dangerous. I will show my Map Square to the other members of the crew and tell them what I know.

Burnley's knowledge

My name is Burnley – Space Officer.

I have seen Map Square 1 made by Andover. Each day we must travel in any of four directions – north, east, south or west. We must watch out for Zitans who would lead us to the Base Area. If we find any roaming Zitans, they are likely to be in sandy areas.

I know about the planet Zita. The climate is hostile. It is hot and very dry. There is no food or water. The only moisture is in the leaves of the trees. We can't eat the leaves and we can't break them off. Even if we could break them off, they would dry up immediately.

If we suck the moisture from the leaves, it will keep us alive for three days. There would be no fourth day without moisture. Today is Day 0, so we must have moisture before Day 4. If we do not have moisture, there will be no fourth day for us.

There is moisture in the trees to the north. It might be a good idea to go north.

Knowledge Cards – continued

Cardiff's knowledge

My name is Cardiff – Space Officer.

I have seen Map Square 1 made by Andover. Our situation is extremely dangerous. We cannot hope for rescue. Our captain is dead. Emergency Regulations state that we can select our own leader if we wish.

We must find Base Area where there is a radio and where Zitans live. We should be able to see the radio mast two days' walk away. Zitans are friendly. They sometimes roam the planet and they prefer to move in sandy areas.

There is no food on Zita, but there is brank. Brank is a sort of stick-like shrub. It contains no moisture but it does have essential minerals. We can break off bits and carry them with us and chew them when we need the minerals.

As we are in good condition we can keep alive without brank for 15 days. There would be no sixteenth day without brank. To keep alive we must get to an area of brank within the first 15 days.

There are not many areas of brank on this planet. It might be a good idea to travel south to the brank on Map Square 24.

I must tell the others what I know.

Dewsbury's knowledge

My name is Dewsbury – Space Officer.

I have seen Map Square 1 made by Andover.

We need moisture from the leaves of trees at least once every three days, counting tomorrow as the first day. But we can't eat the leaves or break them off.

We must have vital minerals from brank at least once every 15 days, counting tomorrow as the first day. We can break off bits of brank and carry them with us.

Even with moisture and minerals we must reach the Base Area within 21 days. Otherwise there would be no twenty-second day for us.

I have made a diary – a 21-Day Diary – so that we can record our movements across this planet. I will write down the type of terrain that we travel through and add any comments that might be helpful.

Today we are on grass. There is more grass to the west and one day beyond that is a hill. We could see more from a hill so perhaps it would be a good idea to go in that direction.

If we reached a hill we might be able to see Base Area.

I must tell the others what I know.

© Ken Jones, *Emotional Games for Training*, Gower Publishing Limited, 2002

Knowledge Cards – continued

Exeter's knowledge

My name is Exeter – Space Officer.

I have seen Map Square 1 made by Andover. I have looked at the 21-Day Diary made by Dewsbury.

Our captain is dead. Emergency Regulations state that we can select our own leader if we wish.

I have a compass, but the magnetic field here is uncertain. We must go only north, south, east or west. We must never go diagonally. We cannot try to take short-cuts to the north-east or south-west and so on.

This planet is volcanic, and it may be unwise to travel on areas of ash.

We must find the Base Area where Zitans live. It has a large radio mast which we could see from two days' walk away.

Zitans are friendly and sometimes roam the planet. They prefer to move on sandy areas so perhaps it would be a good idea to travel east to Map Square 5.

I must tell the others what I know.

Dewsbury's 21-Day Diary

Day	Map Square no.	Type of terrain	Comments
0	*1*	*grass*	
1			
2			
3			
4			
5			
6			
7			
8			
9			
10			
11			
12			
13			
14			
15			
16			
17			
18			
19			
20			
21			

© Ken Jones, *Emotional Games for Training*, Gower Publishing Limited, 2002

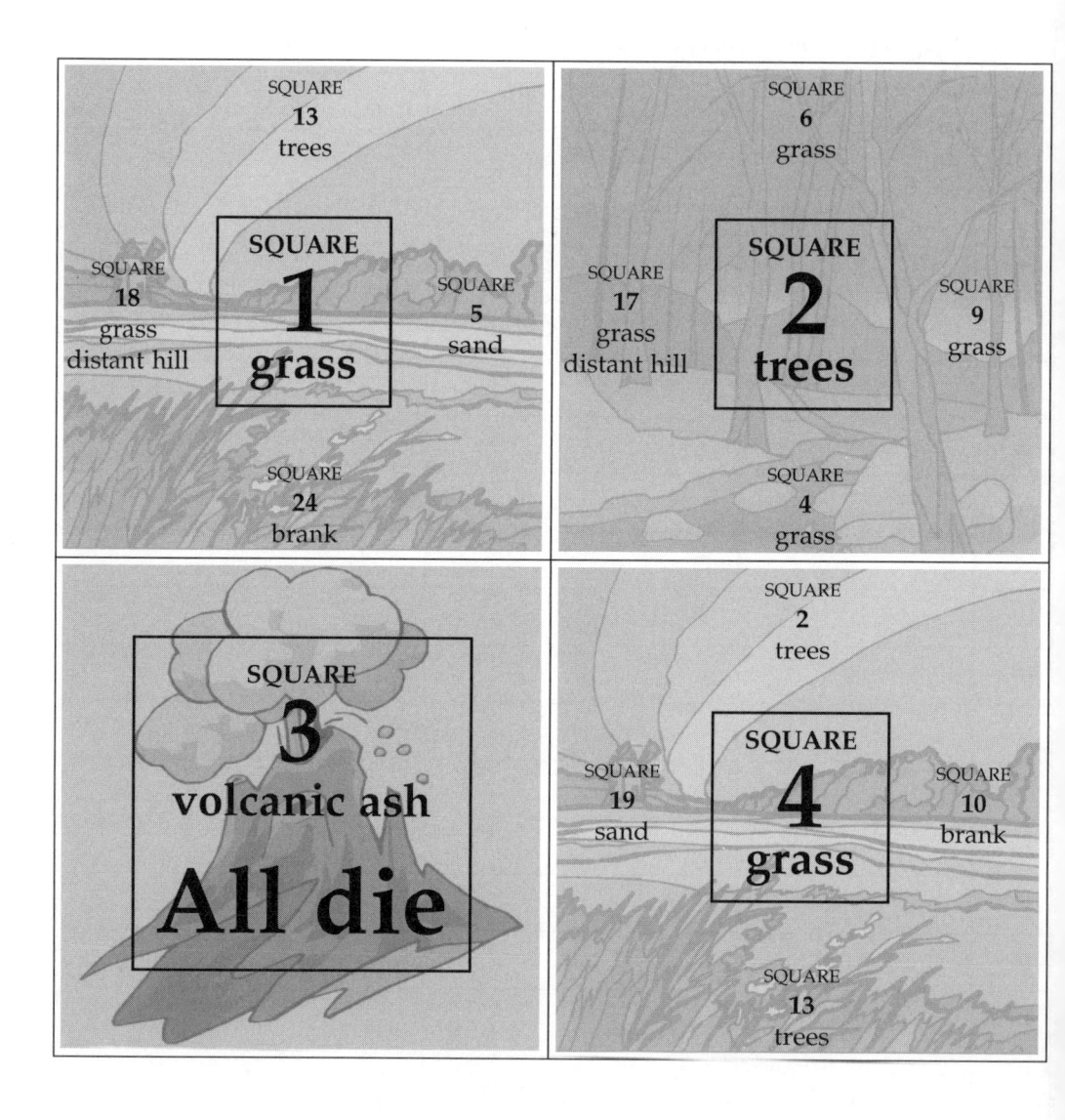

Map Squares – cut out

SQUARE 1 grass
- SQUARE 13 trees
- SQUARE 18 grass distant hill
- SQUARE 5 sand
- SQUARE 24 brank

SQUARE 2 trees
- SQUARE 6 grass
- SQUARE 17 grass distant hill
- SQUARE 9 grass
- SQUARE 4 grass

SQUARE 3 volcanic ash
All die

SQUARE 4 grass
- SQUARE 2 trees
- SQUARE 19 sand
- SQUARE 10 brank
- SQUARE 13 trees

© Ken Jones, *Emotional Games for Training*, Gower Publishing Limited, 2002

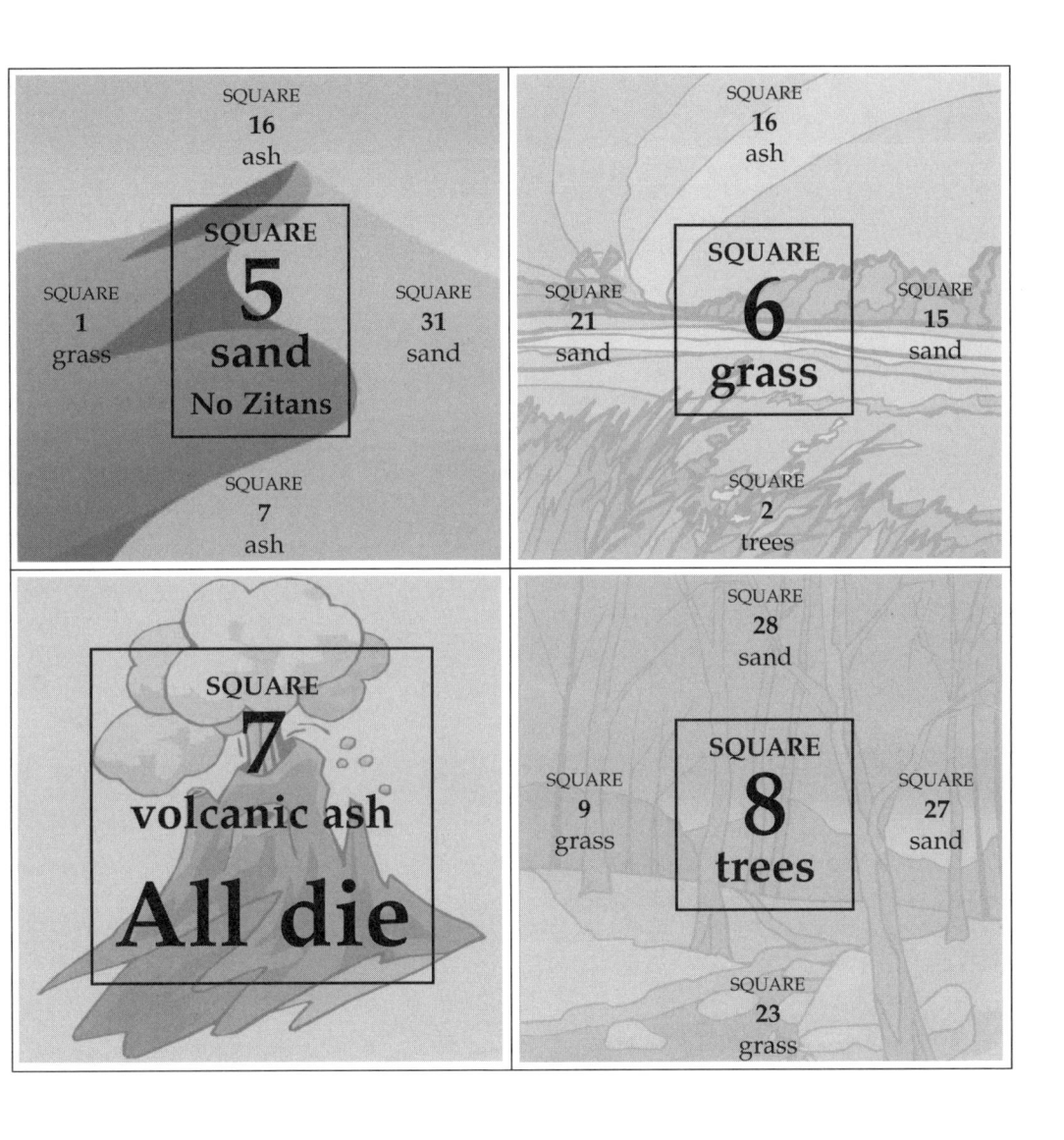

Map Squares – continued

SQUARE 16 ash	SQUARE 16 ash
SQUARE 1 grass — **SQUARE 5 sand No Zitans** — SQUARE 31 sand	SQUARE 21 sand — **SQUARE 6 grass** — SQUARE 15 sand
SQUARE 7 ash	SQUARE 2 trees
—	SQUARE 28 sand
SQUARE 7 volcanic ash All die	SQUARE 9 grass — **SQUARE 8 trees** — SQUARE 27 sand
	SQUARE 23 grass

© Ken Jones, *Emotional Games for Training*, Gower Publishing Limited, 2002

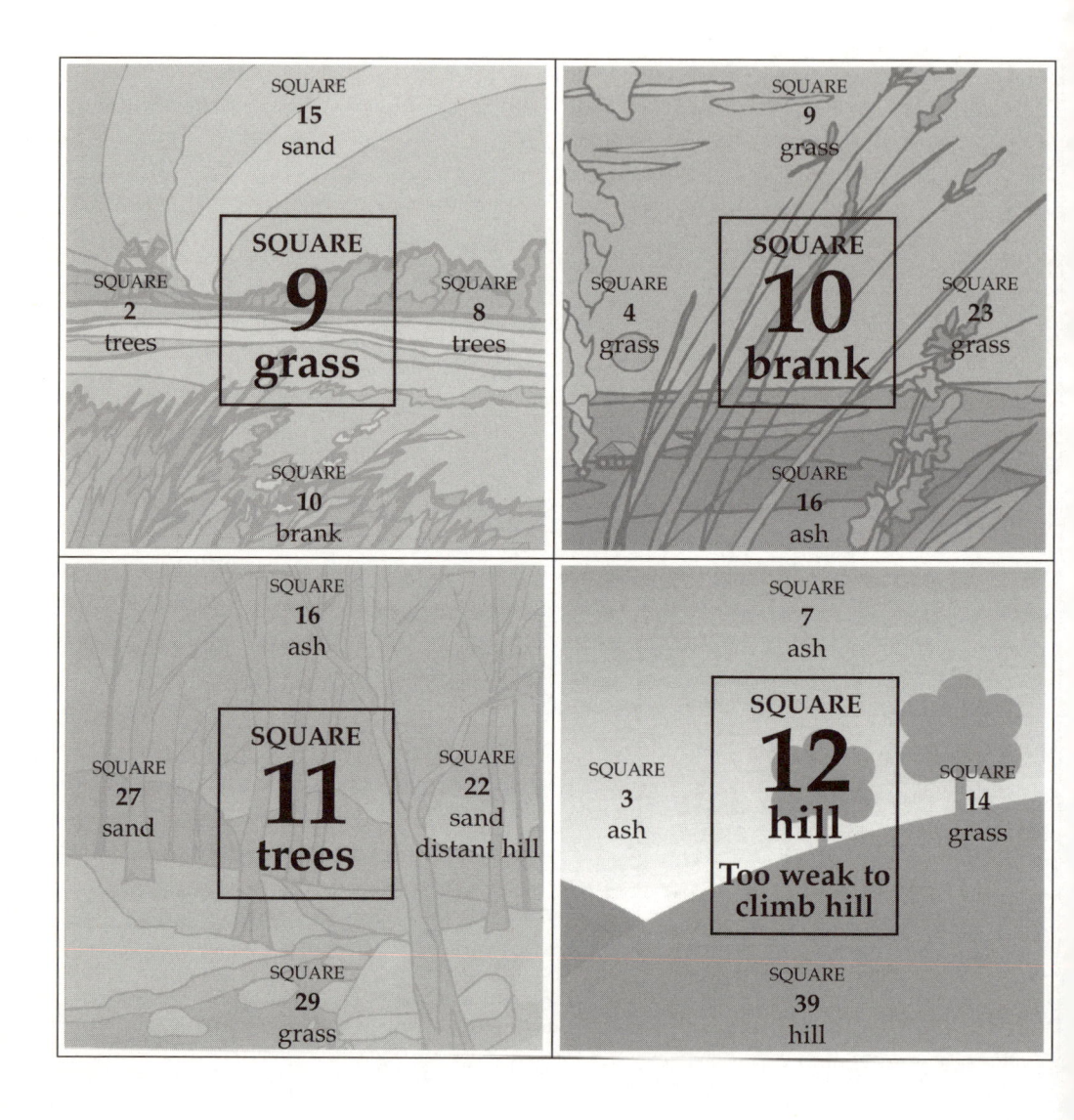

Map Squares – continued

SQUARE 15 sand SQUARE 2 trees — **SQUARE 9 grass** — SQUARE 8 trees SQUARE 10 brank	SQUARE 9 grass SQUARE 4 grass — **SQUARE 10 brank** — SQUARE 23 grass SQUARE 16 ash
SQUARE 16 ash SQUARE 27 sand — **SQUARE 11 trees** — SQUARE 22 sand distant hill SQUARE 29 grass	SQUARE 7 ash SQUARE 3 ash — **SQUARE 12 hill** Too weak to climb hill — SQUARE 14 grass SQUARE 39 hill

© Ken Jones, *Emotional Games for Training*, Gower Publishing Limited, 2002

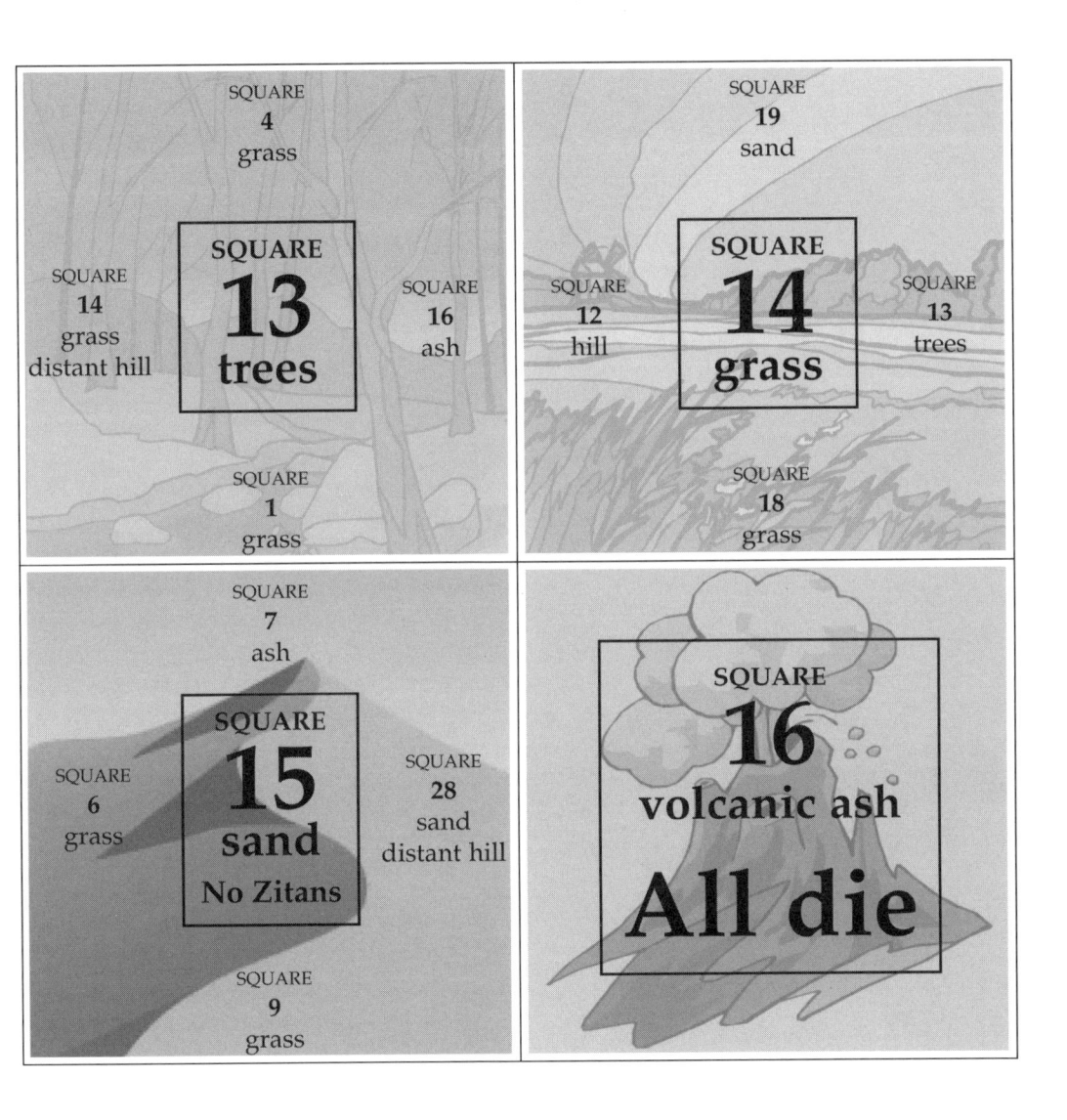

Map Squares – continued

SQUARE 4 grass SQUARE 14 grass distant hill — **SQUARE 13 trees** — SQUARE 16 ash SQUARE 1 grass	SQUARE 19 sand SQUARE 12 hill — **SQUARE 14 grass** — SQUARE 13 trees SQUARE 18 grass
SQUARE 7 ash SQUARE 6 grass — **SQUARE 15 sand — No Zitans** — SQUARE 28 sand distant hill SQUARE 9 grass	**SQUARE 16 volcanic ash — All die**

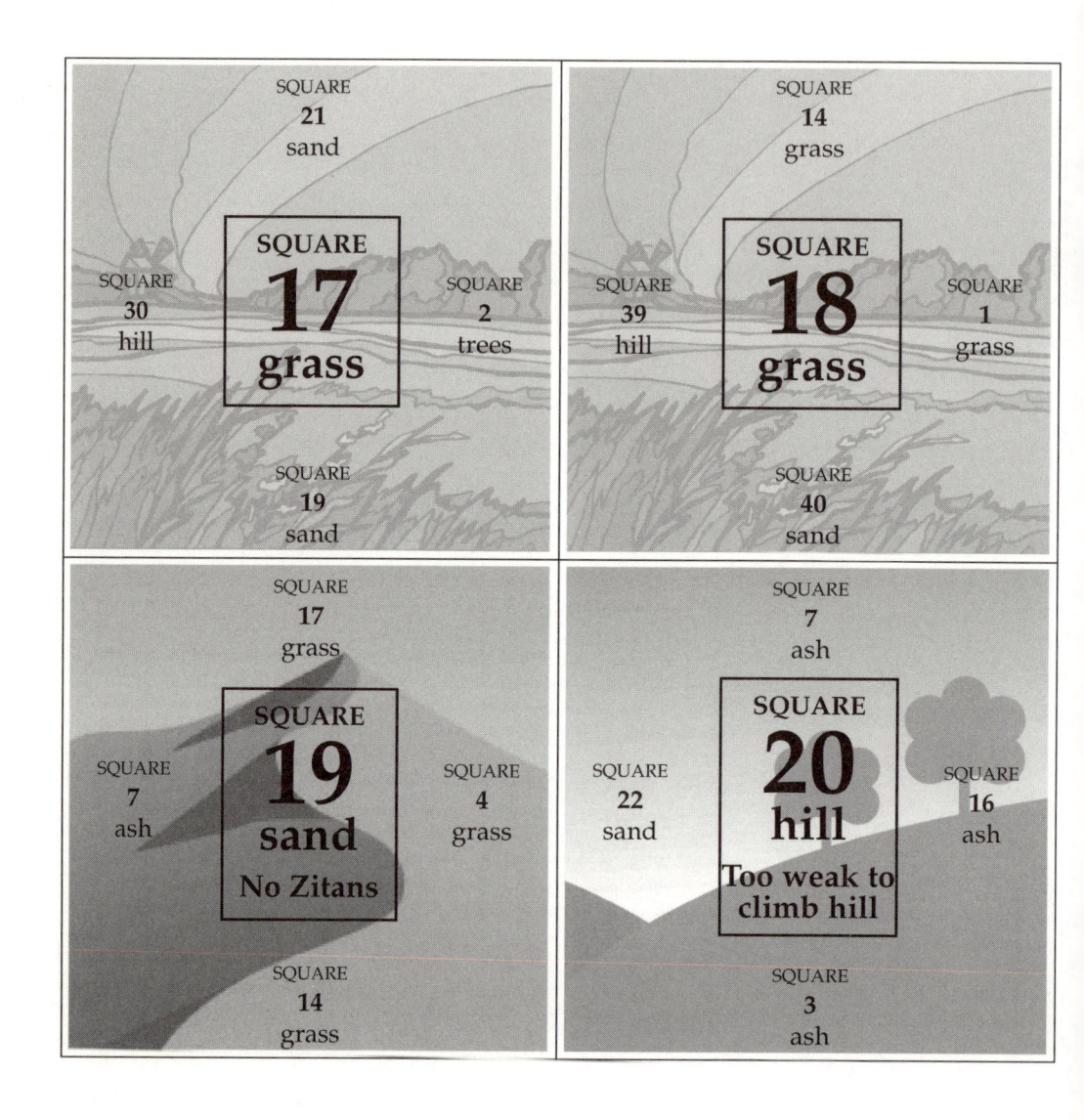

Map Squares – continued

SQUARE 21 sand SQUARE 30 hill — **SQUARE 17 grass** — SQUARE 2 trees SQUARE 19 sand	SQUARE 14 grass SQUARE 39 hill — **SQUARE 18 grass** — SQUARE 1 grass SQUARE 40 sand
SQUARE 17 grass SQUARE 7 ash — **SQUARE 19 sand — No Zitans** — SQUARE 4 grass SQUARE 14 grass	SQUARE 7 ash SQUARE 22 sand — **SQUARE 20 hill — Too weak to climb hill** — SQUARE 16 ash SQUARE 3 ash

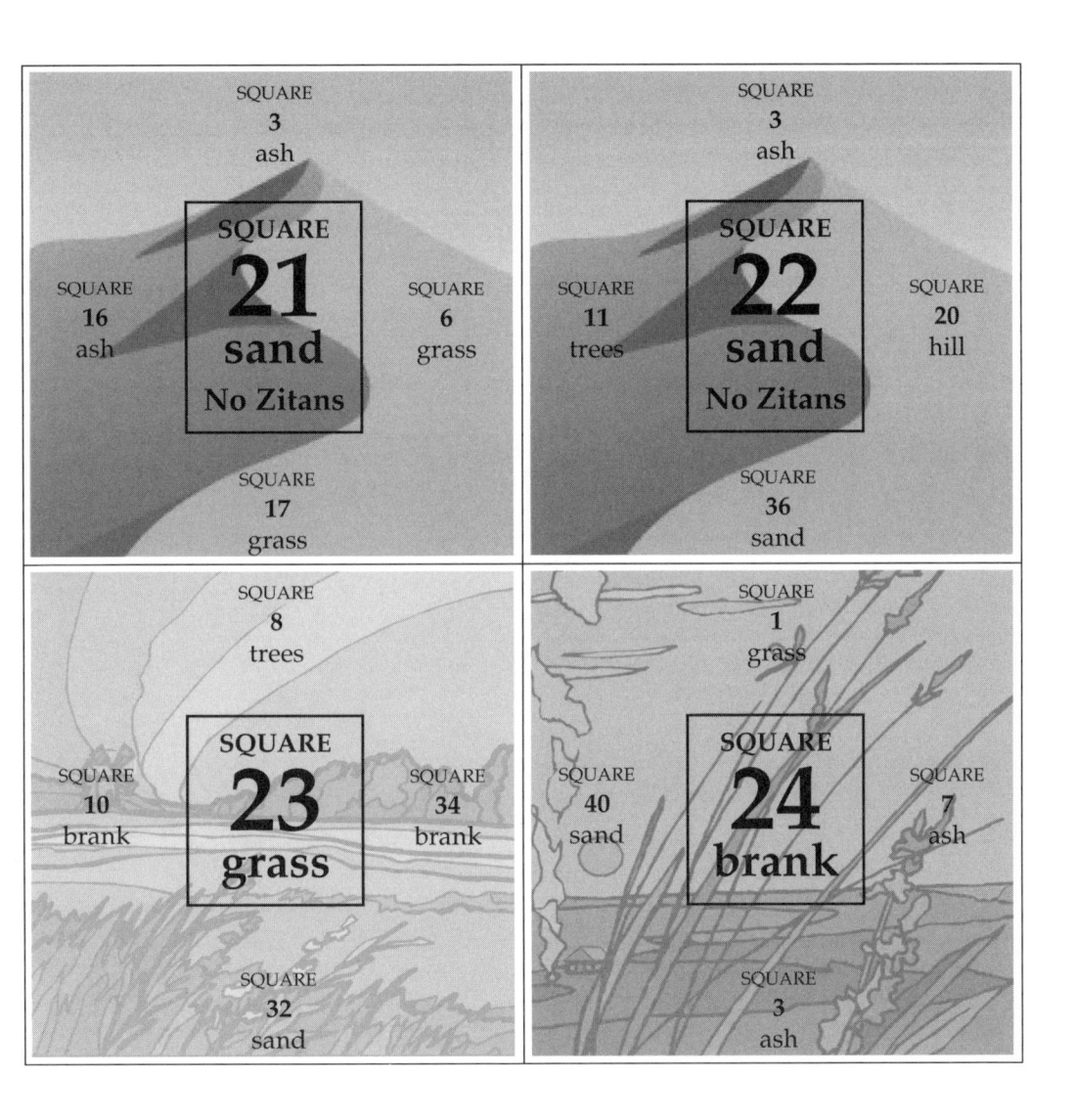

Map Squares – continued

SQUARE 3 ash SQUARE 16 ash — **SQUARE 21 sand No Zitans** — SQUARE 6 grass SQUARE 17 grass	SQUARE 3 ash SQUARE 11 trees — **SQUARE 22 sand No Zitans** — SQUARE 20 hill SQUARE 36 sand
SQUARE 8 trees SQUARE 10 brank — **SQUARE 23 grass** — SQUARE 34 brank SQUARE 32 sand	SQUARE 1 grass SQUARE 40 sand — **SQUARE 24 brank** — SQUARE 7 ash SQUARE 3 ash

© Ken Jones, *Emotional Games for Training*, Gower Publishing Limited, 2002

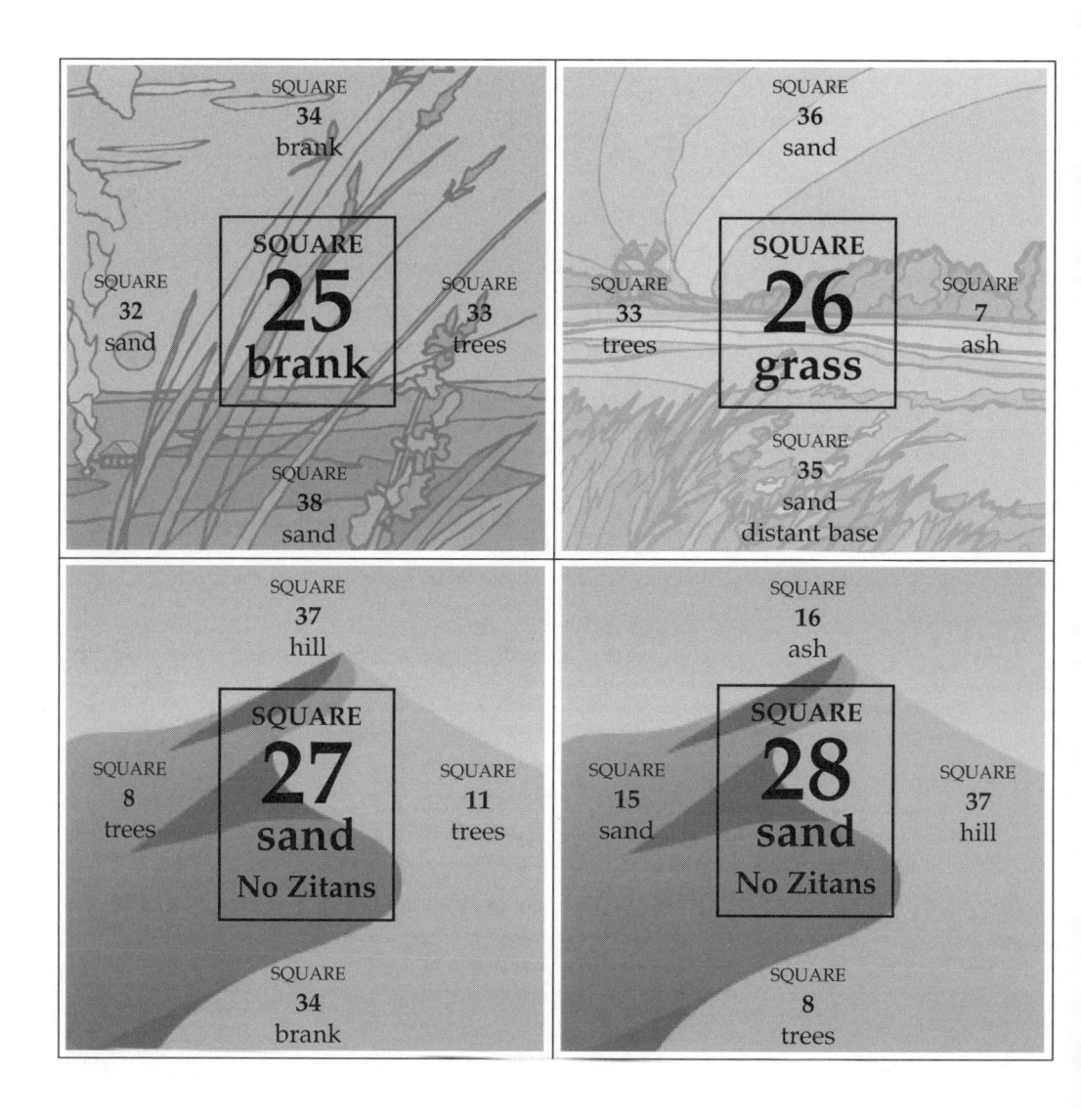

Map Squares – continued

SQUARE 34 brank SQUARE 32 sand — **SQUARE 25 brank** — SQUARE 33 trees SQUARE 38 sand	SQUARE 36 sand SQUARE 33 trees — **SQUARE 26 grass** — SQUARE 7 ash SQUARE 35 sand distant base
SQUARE 37 hill SQUARE 8 trees — **SQUARE 27 sand — No Zitans** — SQUARE 11 trees SQUARE 34 brank	SQUARE 16 ash SQUARE 15 sand — **SQUARE 28 sand — No Zitans** — SQUARE 37 hill SQUARE 8 trees

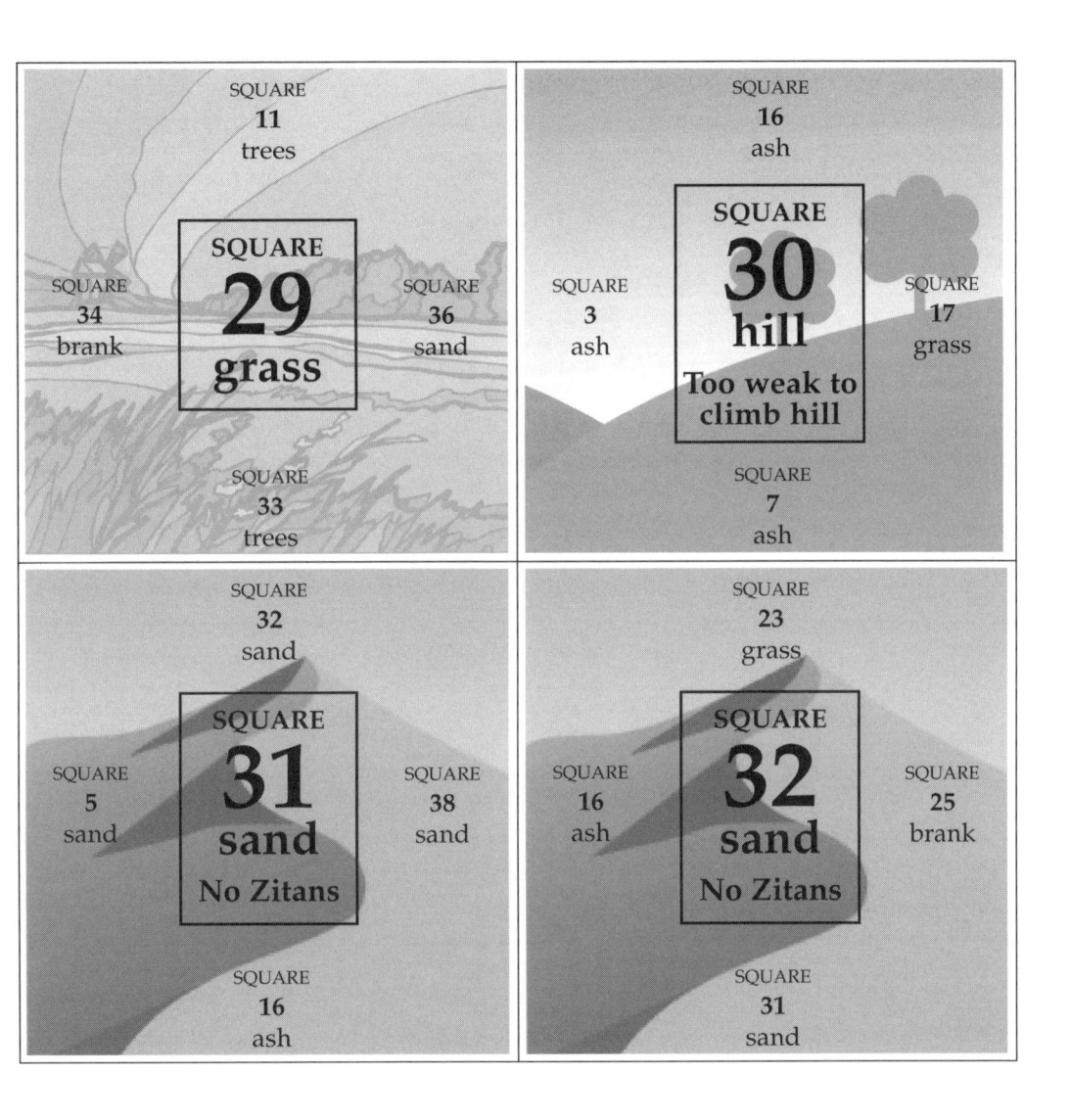

Map Squares – continued

SQUARE 11 — trees SQUARE 34 — brank / SQUARE 29 grass / SQUARE 36 — sand SQUARE 33 — trees	SQUARE 16 — ash SQUARE 3 — ash / SQUARE 30 hill — Too weak to climb hill / SQUARE 17 — grass SQUARE 7 — ash
SQUARE 32 — sand SQUARE 5 — sand / SQUARE 31 sand — No Zitans / SQUARE 38 — sand SQUARE 16 — ash	SQUARE 23 — grass SQUARE 16 — ash / SQUARE 32 sand — No Zitans / SQUARE 25 — brank SQUARE 31 — sand

© Ken Jones, *Emotional Games for Training*, Gower Publishing Limited, 2002

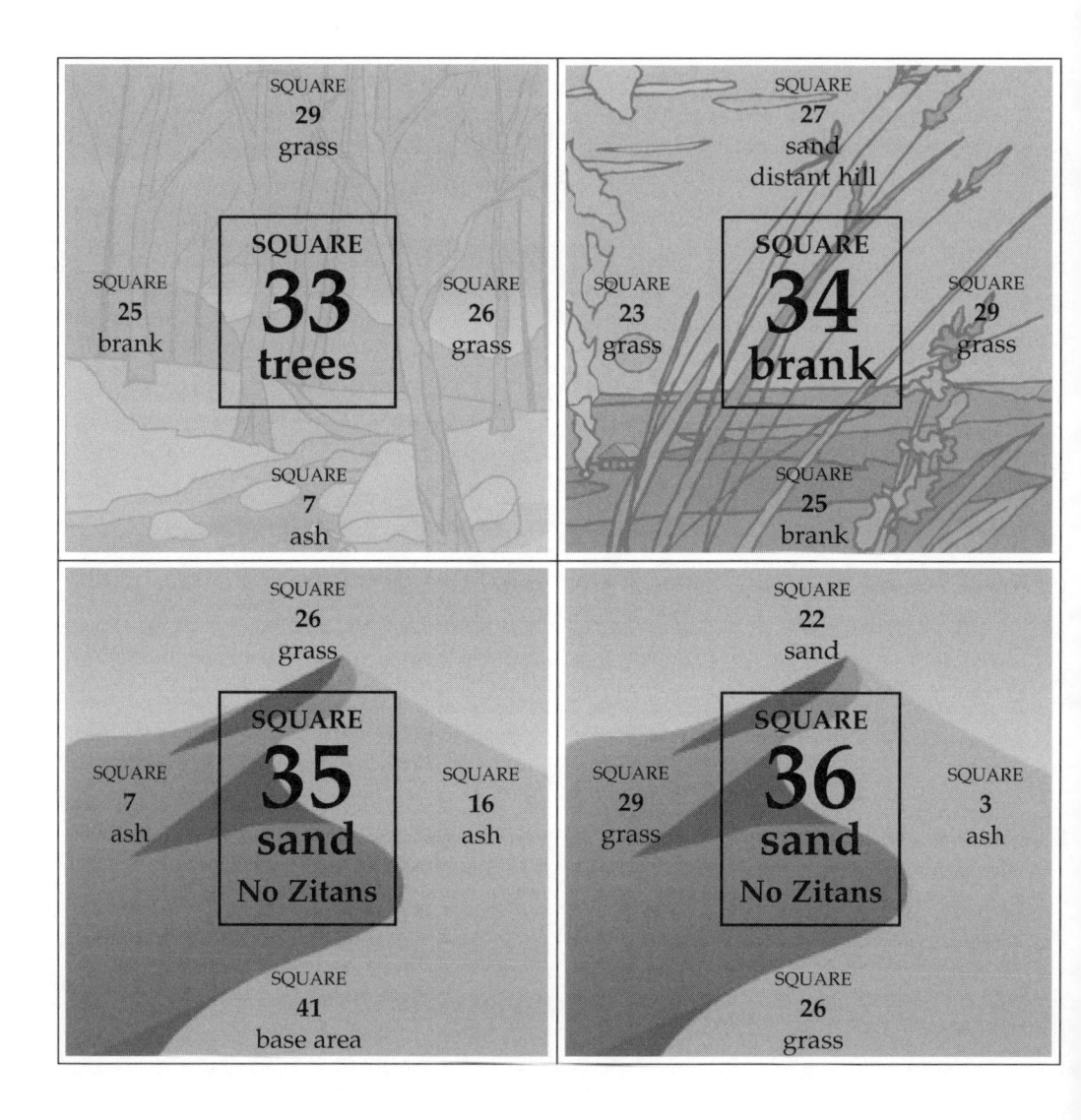

Map Squares – continued

SQUARE 29 grass SQUARE 25 brank — **SQUARE 33 trees** — SQUARE 26 grass SQUARE 7 ash	SQUARE 27 sand distant hill SQUARE 23 grass — **SQUARE 34 brank** — SQUARE 29 grass SQUARE 25 brank
SQUARE 26 grass SQUARE 7 ash — **SQUARE 35 sand No Zitans** — SQUARE 16 ash SQUARE 41 base area	SQUARE 22 sand SQUARE 29 grass — **SQUARE 36 sand No Zitans** — SQUARE 3 ash SQUARE 26 grass

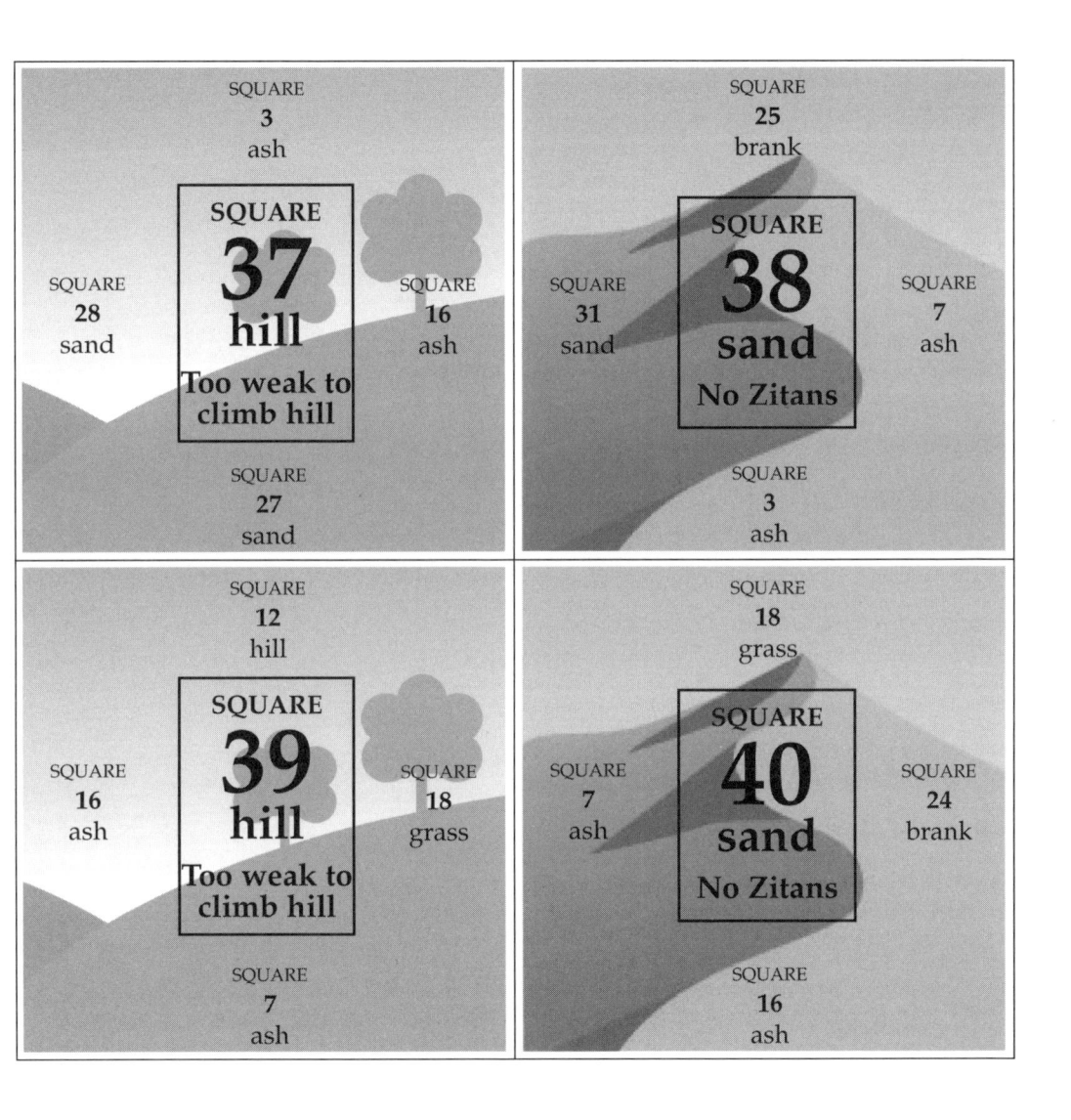

Map Squares – continued

SQUARE 37 hill — Too weak to climb hill
- SQUARE 3 ash
- SQUARE 28 sand
- SQUARE 16 ash
- SQUARE 27 sand

SQUARE 38 sand — No Zitans
- SQUARE 25 brank
- SQUARE 31 sand
- SQUARE 7 ash
- SQUARE 3 ash

SQUARE 39 hill — Too weak to climb hill
- SQUARE 12 hill
- SQUARE 16 ash
- SQUARE 18 grass
- SQUARE 7 ash

SQUARE 40 sand — No Zitans
- SQUARE 18 grass
- SQUARE 7 ash
- SQUARE 24 brank
- SQUARE 16 ash

© Ken Jones, *Emotional Games for Training*, Gower Publishing Limited, 2002

Map Squares – continued

SQUARE
41
Base Area
All safe

6 Interest

Facilitator's Notes

DESCRIPTION

This is a game about the creation of groups and access to groups. Players meet in pairs and can, if they wish, set up an 'interest group' with its own password. Players can also recruit other players into already-formed interest groups. The winner is the player who knows the most passwords.

AIMS

To reveal the sort of emotions associated with belonging and non-belonging, secrecy and openness, and also the emotions associated with getting to know people better.

COMMENTS

This game is easy to run and can be used as an icebreaker. It is also the sort of game which can be interrupted for a break and then resumed, perhaps the following day.

TIME AND NUMBERS

The minimum number of players is about ten. There is no maximum number. If run as an icebreaker with little or no debriefing it might take about half an hour. But, with large numbers and to gain the most benefit from the game, it is best to allow an hour or more.

MATERIALS

- Notes for Participants – one for each player
- Rules of Interest – one for each player
- Meetings Form – one for each player
- Password Record – one for each player
- Identity Cards – one for each player

BRIEFING

Before the event, photocopy the materials for participants and cut out the required number of Identity Cards.
 Hand out the Notes for Participants and also the Rules of Interest

– one copy of each to each player.

Discuss the mechanics of the event – the timing and location. Explain that you will act as Referee if players have doubts about whether an interest is sufficiently specific – see Rule 3.

Taking into account numbers and space, decide with the players whether meetings should have a time limit – for example, five minutes – and, if so, what signal should be given for starting and finishing. This not only makes it easy to arrange for a break between meetings so that the players can fill in their Meetings Forms, it also allows them to find out who is available for their next meeting.

If, on the other hand, the players prefer an informal arrangement, then although this has the benefit of relaxing the procedures, it may lead to them becoming frustrated because they have to wait before being able to meet someone.

Note: one danger of informality is that players may be tempted to try to meet the most attractive, charismatic or powerful of the other players and remain in discussion with them long after their meeting should have broken up.

ACTION

Retrieve the Notes for Participants and hand out the Meetings Forms, Identity Cards and the Password Records. The action should then run itself.

At the end of the game, each player can read out the passwords that they now know, plus the interest group linked with each password.

DEBRIEFING

One characteristic of the emotions aroused by this game is that they will be personal and not related to being in a role. As mentioned in Notes for Participants, the players are expected to be honest but are not expected to disclose any personal matters they wish to keep private.

The emotions are likely to be varied, including the feelings aroused by secrecy and possible duplicity. Did players experience shivers of delight in devising passwords? Were there feelings of togetherness? What were the emotions on discovering coincidences – 'Good heavens, so we both lived in the same street!'? Did they feel that learning about people was more important to them than trying to win?

Interest: Notes for Participants

In this game players meet only in pairs and, at each meeting, they can, if they wish, set up an 'interest group' and devise a password. Once an interest group has been set up, other players can be recruited and told the password. The winner is the player who knows the most passwords. The procedures are given in Rules of Interest.

The game requires you to be honest on matters of interest. The rules imply that the interests you claim must be genuine and not invented in order to find out passwords.

Another implication of the Rules of Interest is politeness. A blunt 'Are you interested in this, this and this?' is not in the spirit of the rules. Meetings should be friendly and courtesies exchanged.

Note the 'Coincidences' column on the Meetings Form. This should not include anything about interest groups but should deal only with coincidental events such as going to the same school, knowing X, having the same birthday, and so on.

Interest

Rules of Interest

1. Enter your name and (briefly) one of your interests on your Identity Card. The aim is to form interest groups and devise passwords for those groups. The player knowing the most passwords at the end of the event is the winner.
2. Meetings must be held in pairs only – never three or more.
3. Players are not allowed to meet someone again until they have met everyone else once. Interest groups must relate to specific interests, not broad ones. For example, 'sport' is not allowed but 'football' is; 'music' is not allowed, but 'Verdi' is. If in doubt, consult the Referee.
4. Only one new interest group may be set up at each meeting. However, players can be recruited into existing interest groups (provided they are genuinely interested in that topic) and told the password for that group.
5. A password must be in two parts – the first being an innocuous question that does not sound like a password and the second being an implausible reply. Both the question and the reply should be brief – not more than three or four words.
6. At the end of a meeting, enter any passwords on your Password Record and enter the name of the player you have just met on the Meetings Form, even if you have met that player before. If there are no coincidences (as distinct from shared interests), then leave that space blank.
7. You are not allowed to ask direct questions about passwords such as 'What passwords do you know?' or 'How many passwords have you got?' Do not show your Password Record to any other player.

© Ken Jones, *Emotional Games for Training*, Gower Publishing Limited, 2002

Meetings Form

Name: _____

I met	Coincidences

Interest

Password Record

Name: _____

Specific interest	Password question	Password reply

Interest

Identity Cards – cut out

Name: _____	Name: _____
One of my interests:	One of my interests:
_____	_____
Name: _____	Name: _____
One of my interests:	One of my interests:
_____	_____
Name: _____	Name: _____
One of my interests:	One of my interests:
_____	_____

© Ken Jones, *Emotional Games for Training*, Gower Publishing Limited, 2002

Interest

Identity Cards – continued

Name: _____	Name: _____
One of my interests: _____	One of my interests: _____
Name: _____	Name: _____
One of my interests: _____	One of my interests: _____

7 Newsroom

Facilitator's Notes

DESCRIPTION

Alpha Television is recruiting journalists from newspapers to work in the News Department. As part of the selection procedure the applicants take part in the simulation of a news broadcast.

AIMS

To reveal the sort of emotions associated with coping with the flow of news stories with a strict deadline.

COMMENTS

The simulation has its own organizers in the role of News Department Executives, and the event is easy to run. The participants are likely to become highly excited.

TIME AND NUMBERS

The minimum number of participants is ten – two Executives and two teams of four journalists – in which case allow about an hour for the event. With more participants there can be more teams. No more than four or five journalists should be in a team.

MATERIALS

- Notes for Participants – one for each participant
- Guidance for Candidates – one for each participant
- Running Order – one for each news team
- Two e-mails – one copy for each news team
- News stories – one set for each team to be handed out gradually
- Identity Cards – one for each news team

BRIEFING

Before the event, photocopy the materials for participants and cut out the required number of Identity Cards making sure that only two Executive Cards are included.

Hand out the Notes for Participants and discuss the mechanics of the event. If there are several teams of journalists there can be the same

© Ken Jones, *Emotional Games for Training*, Gower Publishing Limited, 2002

deadline for all, but teams which do not broadcast first must be prohibited from any further work on their own bulletins.

The resources need not include actual videorecording – it is sufficient, and perhaps appropriate for the test, that the broadcasters sit at a table and imagine the microphones and cameras. In fact, in some circumstances, elaborate equipment can detract from the immediacy and importance of the action.

Retrieve the Notes for Participants and divide the participants into their news teams, perhaps by placing the Identity Cards face down and letting them pick their own. It is a good idea to give teams names – for example, red, blue, green – and participants should enter their team name in the appropriate space on their Identity Card.

Hand out Guidance for Candidates – one to each participant.

Hand out the Running Order – one for each news team.

Remove any clutter that would be inappropriate to a newsroom.

ACTION

When the journalists are ready, the Executives should hand out the two e-mails. After a couple of minutes they should hand out the first news story – 'Flooding', timed at 12.08.

They should then space the handing out of the other stories, according to the time given at the end of each story.

The final news item – 'Train crash', timed 14.49 – should be handed out about five minutes before the deadline (not in the last minute).

DEBRIEFING

Although the emotions and anxieties of precise timing when hundreds of thousands of viewers are supposedly watching are likely to be stressful, being in a position of responsibility and importance is also highly stimulating.

So that the participants can find out what went on within all the teams, it might be useful to go through the stories and ask the teams to comment on each one. What did they feel about the story? Was it important? Was it interesting? Did it have human values?

How did the teams react to the e-mail appeal to leave out deaths and disasters?

Did the teams take the advice to avoid inverted sentences as mentioned in Guidance for Candidates? There are inverted sentences in: 'Zebra crossing', 'Insuring chemistry', 'Southel vandalized', 'Cattle prices', 'Friends' and 'More mice'.

Newsroom: Notes for Participants

As part of its expansion plans, Alpha Television is recruiting journalists from newspapers to work in the Television News Department.

During the selection procedure the applicants take part in a simulation of a news broadcast – the afternoon bulletin 'News at Three', a three-minute news summary. The problem is one of too much news, and the journalists' job is to select, cut and rewrite stories to fit into the three minutes.

You are either an applicant for the job or an executive member of the TV management whose job it is to observe and assess the teams.

The situation is explained in Alpha Television's Guidance for Candidates. This also points out that, after the broadcasts, the Executives can comment on the performance of the teams but that the assessment of individuals takes place later in committee – which is not part of this simulation.

ALPHA TELEVISION
GUIDANCE FOR CANDIDATES

Thank you for applying for a job as journalist in our newsroom. As part of our assessment you will be divided into teams to simulate News at Three – our mid-afternoon news bulletin which lasts for three minutes.

News at Three usually ends with a human-interest piece, or something amusing. It occasionally includes a short letter from listeners, with a brief comment added. Sometimes it includes brief interviews. If you wish, you can have an interview (or two) with members of your own team but these should explain (not sensationalize) the facts given in the news stories.

The news items come from the independent Alpha News Agency and the time the items are received is given at the bottom of each story. You will also receive one or two e-mails addressed specifically to the programme.

Two or more presenters read News at Three. Try to arrange that successive items are read by different members of your team.

If you do not begin the broadcast precisely on time you fail. Do not even think of pleading 'Give us a few seconds, we're not quite ready.' You can come out of the broadcast any time during the final ten seconds but if you over-run, even by a second, you lose marks.

At the end of your broadcasts our Executives will make some immediate comments on the teams, but not on individuals – personal assessments are always considered in committee later.

ADVICE

Do not try to operate as a committee – there are too many stories and too little time. We suggest that you appoint a 'copy-taster' who has first glance at the stories as they arrive. You should also consider appointing a producer who has the final decision.

Consider giving one member of your team the responsibility for time-keeping. If you rehearse reading some stories you will probably find that it takes one minute to read 13 or 14 lines.

Before the broadcast, write down the stories you intend to use in the Running Order and add up the time required. It's a good idea to include one or two short items at the end which can be left out if there is a danger of over-running.

Finally, as you have never worked for radio or television before, it may be worth pointing out that the spoken word has to be treated differently from the written word. Unlike the eye, the ear cannot go backward if a point is missed. Avoid inverted sentences which begin with a quotation and then reveal who is speaking.

ALPHA TELEVISION
RUNNING ORDER

Story	Reading time

ALPHA TELEVISION
E-MAILS

From: Government Legal Department
To: Alpha TV Newsroom
Subject: Amendment

An amendment to the Theft Acts, which was passed by parliament last week, comes into force today and closes a loophole that previously existed in crime involving computers. In cases involving deception, the law now covers deception by a machine as well as deception by a person.

From: Amanda Bigley, Central City
To: Alpha TV Newsroom
Subject: Death and disaster

I like the amusing little news items, but why must you have so many stories about death and disaster? Why not leave these items until the evening news? Your afternoon news programme should be full of the good things in life.

ALPHA NEWS AGENCY

Flooding

Overnight storms have brought flooding in the western areas of Alpha. Several streets in Westingby are under water. Thunder and rainstorms swept across the area and flash floods brought chaos, causing power cuts. There were hundreds of lightning strikes and a school was set on fire. No one was in the building at the time. On the coastal road a car was struck by a falling tree. The occupants were cut free by the rescue services and suffered only a few cuts and bruises.

Time: 12.08

ALPHA NEWS AGENCY

Zebra crossing

'I just love the little foal, stripes and all,' declared Amanda Olafson, 13-year-old daughter of a farmer and his wife who had bought her a pony from the local wildlife park at Westingby which turned out to be pregnant and, surprise surprise, it has just given birth to a hybrid. The young foal has zebra stripes. It appears that, at the wildlife park, the pony had shared a field with a male zebra.

Time: 12.23

ALPHA NEWS AGENCY

Ghosts in the computer

The opening lecture at the annual international symposium hosted by Central City's prestigious High Institute has been devoted to electronic ghosts. The Principal of the Institute, Dr Ahmed, told his audience that a revolution is taking place in the world of physics in which the strange quantum behaviour of extremely small particles is being harnessed at the dawn of a new information age.

Dr Ahmed said that quantum computers get their enormous power from the ghostly behaviour of tiny electrons. They can be thought of as spinning like a ball which spins in both directions at once. In theory, one electron can deal with two numbers – nought and one – while two electrons can carry out a single calculation on four numbers and three electrons can tackle eight numbers simultaneously and so on. Unfortunately, systems in which a number of these ghostly electrons can be manipulated are extremely delicate. A slight influence from outside can destroy the calculations and that is why some quantum computers are so hard to build.

The symposium will last for three days with 14 lectures given by eminent physicists.

Time: 12.40

ALPHA NEWS AGENCY

MORE....MORE....

Ghosts in the computer – 2

Alpha News Agency Science Correspondent writes: Quantum information is an extremely difficult field. Very clever theories and extremely elegant experiments have laid the foundations of what may potentially lead to another information revolution. Some physicists believe that it may never develop that far – that there may be fundamental limits on the number of 'information bits' that can be manipulated. Others are optimistic. In either case, the science is worth pursuing because of its intrinsic interest and its possible benefits, even if they turn out to be relatively modest.

Time: 12.55

ALPHA NEWS AGENCY

MORE....MORE....

Ghosts in the computer – 3

Our correspondent adds that it is important to realize that quantum phenomena are exhibited clearly only on the submicroscopic scale. Quantum behaviour of the type required for computation (and 'teleportation', which is another matter) is exhibited not only by isolated electrons (which would be very difficult to handle in practice) but by atoms, nuclei and by light quanta. The record to date has been five atoms in a magnetic resonance apparatus – the same type of machine used for magnetic resonance imaging – but at very low temperatures and for a very short time. Two or three quantum bits – qubits – of information have been demonstrated in a small number of other experiments across the world.

Time: 12.58

ALPHA NEWS AGENCY

Insuring chemistry

A large insurance company has entered into a new form of partnership to provide a new state-of-the-art building for the Chemistry Department of South Alpha University. The new building will accommodate different branches of chemistry under one roof – organic, inorganic and physical. The Alpha Allstate Insurance Company announces that this is the largest award yet made under the recent government's Public–Private Investment Scheme.

In return for the funds, Alpha Allstate Insurance Company will be granted half the rights to any commercially viable discoveries made by the Chemistry Department. 'This is a wonderful partnership which meets all our needs,' declared the Dean of the Chemistry Department, Mrs Patel, on hearing the news.

Time: 13.26

ALPHA NEWS AGENCY

Alternative health

'Try Homeopathy Week' – a week devoted to showing the benefits of natural remedies rather than drugs – started yesterday in Northam. Mrs Olive Declos, who has written a book on the subject, told a packed meeting that homeopathic medicines are remedies which stimulate the body to heal itself. They are non-toxic, she declared, and anyone can use the treatment which treats each patient as a unique individual and is an alternative to medical drugs which can sometimes have harmful side-effects.

Time: 14.01

ALPHA NEWS AGENCY

Southel vandalized

Southel, with its prestigious university, should be a jewel in Alpha's architectural heritage but it has never been so ugly, says Professor Phillips of the Southel Business School.

'It is as if an army of bulldozers had charged down some of the streets destroying the beautiful buildings. In their place have arisen a clutter of shops that make the city look like any of the other city centres in Alpha,' writes Professor Phillips in the University's Campus Journal.

Professor Phillips, who is Head of the Architecture Department, deplores the damage that has been caused to Alpha's architecture during the past 25 years and calls for stricter measures to preserve the past and control future property development.

Time: 14.07

ALPHA NEWS AGENCY

Cattle prices

There was a brisk trade in pigs at the weekly cattle market at Dorfield. Dairy cattle were also in demand although dealings were somewhat fewer than in the previous week. There was a steady trade in sheep and poultry. 'Business is fairly normal for this time of the year,' declared one dealer.

Dealing would have been brisker had it not been for the interruption which occurred during the break for lunch. Dealers were in the refreshment room when a travelling circus stopped near the cattle market and a lion escaped into the dealing ring. Fortunately, no cattle were in the ring at the time and, after about 20 minutes, the lion was recaptured. There was no damage or casualties but the incident did cause a delay as farmers wanted to make sure that the lion was secure before they released their cattle into the sales ring.

Time: 14.12

Snap Snap Snap   Train Crash

Two goods trains have crashed near Eastville. There are no reports of casualties.

Time: 14.14

ALPHA NEWS AGENCY

Friends

The government has announced a new scheme to support children. At a news conference in Central City, the Minister of the Interior, Mrs Norma Atkinson, said that, under the scheme, understanding adults would visit children in the care of local authorities and in foster homes.

A pilot study had shown that the children welcomed talking to someone who was totally independent of the system and who was on their side. Mrs Atkinson appealed for volunteers to join the scheme. The work will be unpaid but no formal qualifications were required. Applicants would be subject to the normal references, interviews and police checks but, once accepted, the volunteers would be provided with training, support and advice. The scheme would be called the Friends of Children Movement and she appealed for adults to consider joining. 'The work of independent visitors is invaluable,' she declared.

Time: 14.21

ALPHA NEWS AGENCY

Water management

The government is to take bold steps to improve water management. A government Bill introduced today abolishes the system of local water boards managing individual rivers and replaces it with an authority to control all water resources. This authority would ensure the protection of wetlands and other areas which can reduce flooding and store water in times of drought.

Time: 14.26

Correction Correction Correction to Snap Train Crash

For 'goods' read 'passenger'. Delete the word 'no'.

Time: 14.27

ALPHA NEWS AGENCY

More mice

Twenty-three dormice have been released into the wild. This is under the Species Recovery Initiative at Eastville University. Dormice are among Alpha's most threatened animals and their population has been declining for more than a hundred years.

'When the door of their cage was opened they just ran off into the hedges. I hope they will be all right,' said the farmer on whose field the dormice were released.

Time: 14.38

ALPHA NEWS AGENCY

Train crash – replaces snaps

Two passenger trains have crashed head-on at Eastville. An intercity train was in collision with a local passenger train just as it was leaving Eastville Station. Both engines and several carriages were derailed. At least three people are feared dead and as many as 15 are injured. Casualties are being taken to nearby hospitals, and the emergency services have been called to the scene.

The main line is completely blocked and Eastville Station has been closed down. An official investigation into the cause of the accident has begun. 'It was just awful. There was a terrible bang and a grinding of metal. We could see that it was serious. Many people ran on to the lines to try to help the injured,' said Mr Bala, whose house is a few yards from the railway.

Time: 14.49

Identity Cards – cut out

Applicant	Applicant
Name: _____	Name: _____
Team: _____	Team: _____
Applicant	**Applicant**
Name: _____	Name: _____
Team: _____	Team: _____
Applicant	**Applicant**
Name: _____	Name: _____
Team: _____	Team: _____
Alpha Television Executive	**Alpha Television Executive**
Name: _____	Name: _____

8 Happiness Project

Facilitator's Notes

DESCRIPTION

The executives of four departments of PsychoSciences Inc. in the Republic of Alpha are asked to come up with ideas following the complete failure of Professor Pringle's Joy Monitor to measure happiness.

They meet firstly in their own departments – Finance, Sales, Security and Research – then have separate bilateral meetings with the other departments and, finally, all meet together.

AIMS

To reveal the sort of emotions related to corporate planning and the development of innovative ideas.

COMMENTS

Since the procedure of the meetings is clearly defined, the simulation should run itself.

There are no 'right' answers, but someone is bound to come up with the idea that, although Professor Pringle's device fails to measure happiness, it can measure degrees of unhappiness and thus have considerable marketing potential.

TIME AND NUMBERS

The minimum number is eight – two participants in each of the four departments. There is no maximum number. The simulation should last for about an hour, but allow more time with larger numbers. As the meetings are held in stages, it is easy to arrange for breaks and even to continue the event on the following day.

MATERIALS

- Notes for Participants – one for each participant
- Memo – one for each of the four departments
- Happiness Project Failure – one for each of the four departments
- Report Form – one for each of the four departments
- Identity Cards – one for each participant

© Ken Jones, *Emotional Games for Training*, Gower Publishing Limited, 2002

BRIEFING

Before the event, photocopy the materials for participants and cut out the required number of Identity Cards.

Hand out the Notes for Participants and discuss the mechanics of the event.

Use the Identity Cards, face down, to allocate the participants to the four groups. The groups should be located as far apart as possible to avoid eavesdropping. The meetings should have time limits, even informal time limits, to prevent participants having to wait around until other people have finished their discussions.

Retrieve the Notes for Participants and hand out the Memo and the Professor Pringle document – Happiness Project Failure – one copy for each participant. Give each group a copy of the Report Form.

ACTION

When the discussions start you might be asked questions about PsychoSciences Inc. – for example, 'What does the Security Department do?', 'What other research projects are being explored?' and so on. You can either give plausible answers or say that you don't know.

However, if your answer to a question could have any bearing on discussions in the other groups, then you should keep them informed of the 'facts' of the situation.

DEBRIEFING

The best starting point is for each group to say what they discussed in private. From this it will probably be clear that the emotions aroused were deeper than might be expected. For example, did any group seek to further its own interest by concealing their bright ideas in order to reveal them later to the Directors and thereby get the credit?

Assuming that someone came up with the idea that the failed Joy Monitor could be a highly profitable venture for measuring unhappiness did they become elated and filled with a desire to announce the discovery to the world? Or did they plan to swear everyone to secrecy while they approached the security services of their own and possibly other governments?

Basically, what emotions emerged on discovering that they were sitting on a pot of gold?

Happiness Project: Notes for Participants

You are Executives of four departments of PsychoSciences Inc. in the Republic of Alpha and you are asked to come up with ideas following the complete failure of Professor Pringle's Joy Monitor.

The Directors envisage the possibility of staff redundancies and ask you to discuss the situation. Details of specific jobs that could be cut are not available but you can assume that each of the four departments could be downsized by about 10 per cent of the workforce, including Executives.

In order to cover the options, they wish you to meet firstly within your own department – Finance, Sales, Security and Research – to see if you can offer any cost-cutting ideas. We are providing each department with a Report Form to allow you to jot down any comments, suggestions and proposals.

The second stage is one of bilateral consultations with other departments, so that each department will have three consultation meetings.

The third stage is a joint meeting of all four departments.

© Ken Jones, *Emotional Games for Training*, Gower Publishing Limited, 2002

PsychoSciences Inc.

Memorandum

From: Board of Directors
To: Finance, Sales, Security and Research Departments

As you will see from the enclosed report, the Happiness Project has been aborted. The machine does not work. Professor Pringle has offered his resignation.

Since the project was the central plank of our hope for expansion, we may have to consider not only ceasing recruitment but also reducing our workforce.

Some of our existing projects are approaching their sell-by dates. We would like you to consider which departments could lose staff.

The Directors feel that the best way forward is through departmental initiatives. To this end, we ask you to meet within your departments to see if you can come up with any useful ideas. Then each department should have three separate meetings with the other three departments to try to gain some support for their suggestions.

Finally, all four departments should meet together to put forward ideas about where we should go from here.

Good luck!

PsychoSciences Inc.

HAPPINESS PROJECT FAILURE
by Professor Pringle

1. The Happiness Project was based on my invention of a Joy Monitor.
2. This prototype was tested and has completely failed to achieve its purpose – to monitor happiness.
3. The device was a lightweight hand-held machine looking something like a camcorder. It could have been disguised as some other object had the tests succeeded. It would have been relatively inexpensive to manufacture.
4. The aim was to measure the level of a person's happiness when focused on that person. It was designed to operate at distances of up to 20 metres.
5. The focusing succeeded, but happiness was not recorded at all.
6. Instead the device merely measured unhappiness from disquiet up to a level of potential violence. (We tested it at football matches.)
7. This extremely disappointing result was the exact opposite of what I had been hoping for.
8. I must apologize personally for all the wasted time, money and labour expended on this project, and I hereby offer my resignation.

PsychoSciences Inc.

REPORT FORM
Department: _____
Report:

Identity Cards – cut out

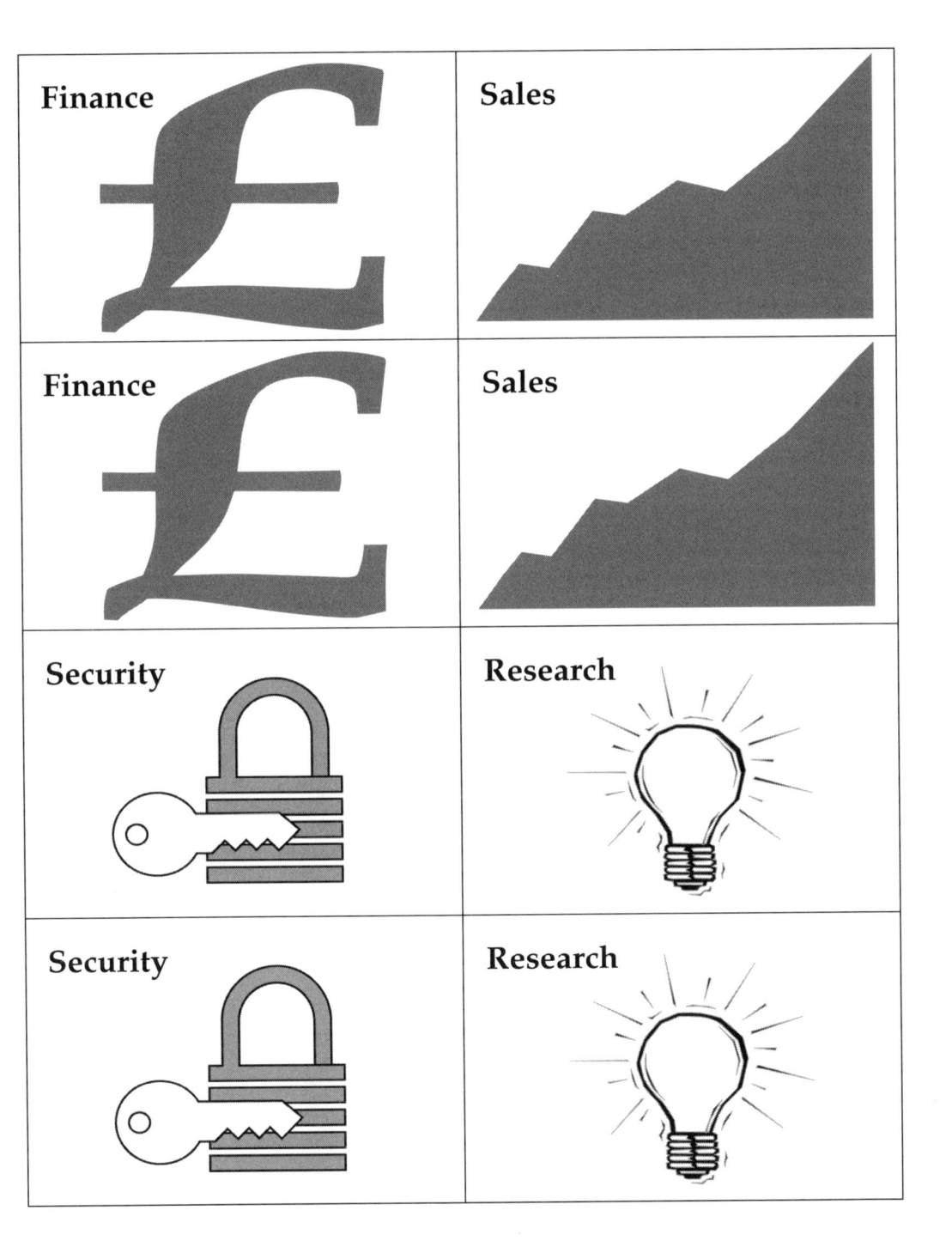

Finance	Sales
Finance	Sales
Security	Research
Security	Research

© Ken Jones, *Emotional Games for Training*, Gower Publishing Limited, 2002

9 Secrecy

Facilitator's Notes

DESCRIPTION

Alpha Allstate Insurance Company Inc. in the Republic of Alpha is holding a series of informal meetings in one of its hospitality suites to discuss ways of preventing computer fraud.

Unbeknown to the company, the Security Manager has committed fraud and is using the interviews with experts to try to find the information that would help cover up the crime. Each person, except the Finance Manager, has confidential information about computer fraud.

AIMS

To reveal the sort of emotions associated with secrecy (and duplicity).

COMMENTS

The key role in this event is that of the Security Manager who is trying to cover up the crime. It seems that there is no need to select a particular person for this role – the event has been run in a variety of situations (including secondary school pupils and international bankers) and no problem seems to have arisen about random role allocation.

TIME AND NUMBERS

The minimum number of participants is six – the Security Manager, the Finance Manager and the four Systems Analysts.

If you have a large number of participants the event can be run in separate groups of six. If the number is not divisible by six, participants could be allocated roles as observers or assistant facilitators or they could share a joint role of Systems Analyst, working together and not splitting up.

The running time depends partly on the participants' experience. Normally, one to two hours is sufficient. Since the simulation has an informal structure it is easy to arrange for breaks during the action.

MATERIALS

- Notes for Participants – one copy for each participant
- Memorandum from the Board of Directors – one copy for each participant

- Record of Meetings Form – one for each participant
- Identity Cards – one for each participant
- Knowledge Cards (confidential) – one for each participant

BRIEFING

Before you run this simulation, photocopy the materials for participants and cut out the required number of Identity and Knowledge Cards. Then decide on the location of the hospitality suite. Is it the classroom, corridor, garden, staffroom, restaurant or are there several possible locations? Also consider the possibility of actual refreshments – coffee, cakes, and so on.

Hand out the Notes for Participants and the Memorandum – one for each participant.

Discuss the timing and whether there should be breaks in the action. Retrieve the Notes for Participants and remove any clutter that would not be present in the hospitality suite.

Attach the Identity Cards to the appropriate Knowledge Cards and allocate them at random, perhaps placing them face down and asking the participants to choose their own.

It is absolutely vital that the Knowledge Cards should be kept secret and not revealed inadvertently. (Note: this is particularly important in the case of the Security Manager.)

Finally, hand out the Record of Meetings Forms.

Do not give any hints that fraud has actually occurred.

ACTION

The simulation will probably run itself.

If there are two or more simulations being run simultaneously and one group finishes well ahead of the others, discuss with the group what they should do. Should they become observers, go for a coffee, help you, or prepare for and run the debriefing?

DEBRIEFING

If the event was run as several separate simulations it might be a good idea for each group to hold their own mini-debriefing and then report their findings at a general meeting of all participants.

The first stage should be an exchange of Knowledge Cards so that everyone sees the information possessed by the others. This is particularly important in the case of the Security Manager.

The emotions associated with secrecy tend to be complicated. Often there is a mixture of guilt and excitement. Added to this are the emotions associated with professional ethics – how does one feel about duty to oneself, one's colleagues and one's employers when in possession of secret information? And what were the emotions of anyone who wondered whether to earn some money by leaking the story of the defective security system to the media?

Note: The Security Manager's task is to find the name of two animals whose initial letters follow each other alphabetically. The animals are: giraffe, hyena, impala and jackal, giving three possible codes – giraffehyena, hyenaimpala, and impalajackal. Finding out the name of two of the animals would give a 50 per cent chance of success and finding out three would guarantee it. However, for the codes to work there must be no space or hyphen between the names of the two animals. The Security Manager is fairly sure there is a hyphen between the names, but all four Systems Analysts know that there is no hyphen.

Secrecy: Notes for Participants

Alpha Allstate Insurance Company Inc. is holding meetings in one of its hospitality suites to discuss ways of avoiding computer fraud.

You are a member of the company and you will receive a memo from the Board of Directors inviting you to the meeting and explaining the purpose and procedures.

As explained in the memo, it is possible that you may not know everyone else in the meetings, so wear your Identity Card.

In addition, you will have a personal and confidential Knowledge Card. When you have read it, conceal it. If you need to look at it again, do so privately.

ALPHA ALLSTATE INSURANCE COMPANY INC.

Memorandum

From: the Board of Directors
To: Abingdon, Finance Manager,
Bexley, Security Manager
Chester, Dover, Edinburgh and Farnham, Systems Analysts

We have pleasure in inviting you to a series of one-to-one meetings in the relaxed atmosphere of one of our hospitality suites for a frank exchange of opinions on the question of our computer security. The issues to be discussed are as follows:

- Computer security is a matter of increasing concern.
- We are probably well protected against outside hacking.
- We need to strengthen our defences against internal fraud.

You should meet only one other person at a time so that you can talk in confidence. Try not to meet the same person for a second time until you have met everyone else once.

You may not know everyone at these meetings, so please wear your Identity Card. We will provide you with a Record of Meetings Form.

After meeting in pairs, get together as a group to see if you can make any recommendations about ways to improve security.

ALPHA ALLSTATE INSURANCE COMPANY INC.

Record of Meetings Form
(Do not record any confidential information on this form)

Name: _____

Person met	Subject discussed

Identity Cards – cut out

Abingdon Finance Manager	**Bexley** Security Manager
Chester Systems Analyst	**Dover** Systems Analyst
Edinburgh Systems Analyst	**Farnham** Systems Analyst

© Ken Jones, *Emotional Games for Training*, Gower Publishing Limited, 2002

Knowledge Cards – cut out

Abingdon's knowledge

CONFIDENTIAL

Obviously, the Security Manager and myself will not ask technical questions about computers. This is not a job interview, and our Systems Analysts are experts in their field.

Our task, as far as I see it, is to:

- see who can come up with good ideas, and
- consider whether any of them could be candidates for promotion in the future. For example, if some sort of team is set up, it will probably need a leader.

My worry is that I am not convinced that our present system is completely secure. For all I know, some degree of computer fraud may be going on now. If fraud is taking place, probably anyone at the meeting could be a suspect – except myself, of course, because I know that I have not committed fraud.

Bexley's knowledge

CONFIDENTIAL

I don't know why I did it. This is my first crime – and my last.

Perhaps it was because my investments collapsed. Maybe it was because my job is dull and I wanted some adventure, some danger. Whatever the reason, I did it.

I used my computer knowledge to set up a fictitious account and transferred company money into the account – about the equivalent of my annual salary. Then I withdrew the money.

Unfortunately, I cannot find the code I need to bury the transaction for ever. I know that there is at least one such code containing the name of two animals in alphabetical order, with the initial letter of the second animal one place further down the alphabet than the first animal. So I am looking for something like 'antelope-bison', or 'cat-dog', but not 'dog-cat' or 'cat-elephant'. I'm pretty sure that the two names have a hyphen between them.

The System Analysts may know the code. If I cannot get them to tell me, I could try to bribe them. Bribing with money could be dangerous, but I could offer them promotion, possibly to Overseas Operations – a chance for them to see the world.

Knowledge Cards – continued

Chester's knowledge

CONFIDENTIAL

Although the other Systems Analysts may not have realized this, the company's computer system is insecure. Fraud may be taking place.

I have discovered that there is a code that could be used to cover up fraud in the computer system. The code is the name of two animals joined together. There is no hyphen or space between the two names.

I know half of one of the codes – it is giraffe.

I realize that this is highly secret information.

I would very much like to work in Central Division or in Overseas Operations.

Dover's knowledge

CONFIDENTIAL

Although the other Systems Analysts may not have realized this, the company's computer system is insecure. Fraud may be taking place.

I have discovered that there is a code that could be used to cover up fraud in the computer system. The code is the name of two animals joined together. There is no hyphen or space between the two names.

I know half of one of the codes – it is hyena.

I realize that this is highly secret information.

I would very much like to work in Central Division or in Overseas Operations.

Knowledge Cards – continued

Edinburgh's knowledge

CONFIDENTIAL

Although the other Systems Analysts may not have realized this, the company's computer system is insecure. Fraud may be taking place.

I have discovered that there is a code that could be used to cover up fraud in the computer system. The code is the name of two animals joined together. There is no hyphen or space between the two names.
I know half of one of the codes – it is impala.
I realize that this is highly secret information.
I would very much like to work in Central Division or in Overseas Operations.

Farnham's knowledge

CONFIDENTIAL

Although the other Systems Analysts may not have realized this, the company's computer system is insecure. Fraud may be taking place.

I have discovered that there is a code that could be used to cover up fraud in the computer system. The code is the name of two animals joined together. There is no hyphen or space between the two names.
I know half of one of the codes – it is jackal.
I realize that this is highly secret information.
I would very much like to work in Central Division or in Overseas Operations.

10 Creating Events

Facilitator's Notes

DESCRIPTION

Creative Activities Inc. in the Republic of Alpha is running a selection procedure for people applying for jobs in the Editorial Department. The applicants try to devise a game or simulation relating to business ethics (or lack of ethics) and then present their ideas in a creative way.

AIMS

To reveal the sort of emotions involved in creative thinking about the structures of games and simulations involving business ethics. Since ethics involve emotions, it should reveal how the participants feel about honesty, loyalty, cheating, and so on.

The presentations, which can include drama, are also likely to elicit a variety of emotions.

COMMENTS

The action is straightforward with strict procedures. But imaginations are not inhibited and all sorts of games and simulations – from the practical to the fantastic – can emerge. The emotions develop progressively with the flow of ideas and tend to progress from doubt to enthusiasm.

The Executives can tackle any procedural problems, leaving you, as the facilitator, with plenty of opportunities for observing what is going on.

Consider what you would do if the participants request that you run the game or simulation which is considered the most creative by the Executives – or even that you run all of the creative events.

TIME AND NUMBERS

Normally, one hour is sufficient to complete the event but, with large numbers of participants, it is better to allow two hours and incorporate a break or two so that the participants can consider their options.

A time limit should be set for each stage – 10 to 20 minutes or so for each of the first three stages. The time allowed for the presentations will depend on the number of participants.

The minimum number of participants is seven – three pairs of

Creating Events

applicants plus an Executive. The maximum number depends only on the amount of space and time available.

MATERIALS

- Notes for Participants – one copy for each participant
- Advice Sheet – one copy for each team, plus a copy for each Executive
- Creativity Forms – one set of four for each team
- Resources for presentations – flipcharts, coloured pens, overhead projectors, audiocassette recorders, music and so on

BRIEFING

Before the event, photocopy the materials for participants.

Hand out the Notes for Participants, and divide the participants randomly into teams, including an Executive team.

Discuss the mechanics of the event – the timing, the locations of the teams and presentation areas, and the resources available.

Also discuss how the ideas should be passed around at each stage. Should every team pass their ideas on to every other team – perhaps going round in a circle – or should the ideas go back and forwards between two teams?

It is advisable to set a deadline for each stage – this avoids the situation in which one team is waiting impatiently for another team to finish.

Retrieve the Notes for Participants and remove any clutter that is inappropriate to the situation from the area.

Hand out the Advice Sheet and the sets of forms relating to the stages – one copy to each team.

ACTION

The action is straightforward and, if some participants are taking the role of Executives, there will be plenty of opportunities to observe what is happening – who is talking to whom, who is taking the role of leader, who is getting excited, and so on.

It is probably advisable to discuss with the Executives the way in which they propose to organize the presentations, including the available resources – such as flipcharts.

DEBRIEFING

It may be a good idea for each group (including the Executives if there is more than one) to hold their own mini-debriefing about the emotions involved and then report their findings at a general meeting of all participants.

Since ethics is the subject of the games and simulations, what emotions arose and how were they handled? Were there arguments? What did they discuss in terms of such issues as loyalty, theft, lies and cheating in a business environment?

Also, what emotions were aroused relating to the presentations – not only on the part of the presenters but also on the part of the audience?

Creating Events: Notes for Participants

Creative Activities Inc. in the Republic of Alpha is running a selection procedure for people applying for jobs in the Editorial Department. You are either an applicant or an Executive of the company.

The selection procedure includes an activity in which teams try to devise a game or simulation relating to business ethics (or lack of ethics).

Each team will have a copy of the Advice Sheet which Creative Activities Inc. hands out to applicants. This describes the procedures.

In addition, each team will have forms for the stages of developing ideas, and these are passed round so that other teams can make comments and suggestions.

Finally, it is your task to present your ideas to the Executives and the other teams, and to do this creatively.

Creative
Activities INC.

ADVICE SHEET

The task set for each team is to design a game or simulation about a situation involving business ethics, or lack of ethics. The task is done in stages in which you decide:

1. what the event is about
2. what are the roles
3. what the participants have to do and what they have to do it with.

At the end of each stage, you should make comments and suggestions about the other teams' ideas and they should do the same for your ideas. Write down the details of your completed event on the Final Form of Completion and show this to the Executives before your presentation.

We are looking for creativity and cooperation. Although you will be in teams, you will not be in competition. We will not be impressed if one team tries to sabotage another team's ideas. We *will* be impressed if teams support each other, particularly in their presentations which we hope will be met with applause, not jeers.

We realize that this stage-by-stage procedure is not the normal process for creating games and simulations, but it does give us an opportunity to see where your strengths lie in creating ideas, organizing procedures, devising explanations and giving presentations.

We will, of course, be particularly interested in your presentations. Make them appropriate and make them creative. You can use whatever resources are available. You do not have to be dramatic, go in for play-acting or even use music, but you may make use of any of these if you wish.

After the presentations our Executives will be happy to give their own comments, but the selection of individuals will take place only when the results of all our assessment procedures and interviews are reviewed later in the week.

Good luck. Enjoy creativity.

Creative Activities INC.

Creativity Form: Stage 1
Team members:
Title of game or simulation:
What is it about? (*Situation/problem related to business ethics*)
Comments from other teams:

Creative Activities INC.

Creativity Form: Stage 2
(Attach this to the Stage 1 document)

What are the roles? *(Duties, functions, responsibilities, and so on)*

Comments from other teams:

$\mathcal{C}$reative
$\mathcal{A}$ctivities INC.

Creativity Form: Stage 3
(*Attach this to the Stages 1 and 2 documents*)

What do the participants have to do? (*Discuss, compete, manufacture, plan*)

What do they do it with? (*Computers, documents, matchsticks*)

Comments from other teams:

Creative Activities INC.

Creativity Form: Stage 4 – Completion
Team members:
Title of game or simulation:
Description:

11 Feeling Virtuous

Facilitator's Notes

DESCRIPTION

This is a game in which the objective is to make the most accurate guess about the ranking order of the virtues chosen by all the participants.

The virtues are justice, truth, beauty, humour, faith, hope and charity. At the end of discussions between pairs, each participant must vote for three of the seven virtues (in no special order). Each player must also guess (in ranking order) the three virtues that are most valued by the other players.

AIMS

To reveal the sort of emotions connected with virtues – in terms of both personal values and the values of other people.

COMMENTS

This game is easy to run and penetrates areas which are not normally explored. Values do matter, and participants can learn a great deal from each other about basic issues, which could be both interesting and enlightening.

TIME AND NUMBERS

The minimum number of participants is probably about ten, in which case the event might last up to an hour. With larger numbers allow more time.

MATERIALS

- Notes for Participants – one for each participant
- Meetings Form – one for each participant
- Predictions Form – one for each participant
- Identity Cards – one for each participant
- Virtue Cards – one set for each participant

BRIEFING

Before the event photocopy the materials for participants and cut out the required number of Identity and Virtue Cards.

Hand out the Notes for Participants and discuss the mechanics of the event. One key issue is the timing of meetings of the pairs (meetings of three or more are not allowed). It is useful to agree on a time limit and that a signal be given for people to change pairs. This not only avoids one or two pairs extending their meetings for personal reasons, but also gives participants the opportunity to do their paperwork.

Specify an area, or areas, for the meetings – this could be a corridor or any other suitable space.

To preserve privacy try to organize two ballot boxes for the voting – one for the three selected virtues and the other for the four discarded virtues. Enlist some help for counting the votes and placing the popular choices in order.

Retrieve the Notes for Participants and hand out a set of the seven Virtue Cards to each participant.

Give each participant a Meetings Form, a Predictions Form and an Identity Card.

ACTION

The game should run itself, particularly if you have agreed on a deadline for each round of meetings. If, during the game, the participants find that the time allowed for each meeting is too short or too long, then you can alter the timings.

Respect the privacy of the vote, since participants may have lied about their voting intentions.

DEBRIEFING

You could begin by asking the participants whether they were surprised by the result of the vote. Any surprising finding is interesting and worth discussing.

Follow up by asking what sort of personal qualities would help a participant win the game.

What emotions were felt in the game? Did players feel open or secretive? Were players happy to discuss the merits of the respective virtues or did they feel uncomfortable? How friendly were the encounters? Was there support and understanding? Were there arguments? What was the general tone of the meetings?

Feeling Virtuous: Notes for Participants

This is a game in which the object is to make the most accurate guess about the ranking order of the virtues chosen by all the players in the game.

The seven virtues in the game are justice, truth, beauty, humour, faith, hope and charity. Each player will receive seven Virtue Cards and, at the end of the game, must vote for three of the seven (in no special order) as being the most valuable and discard the other four cards. Each player must also guess (in ranking order) the three virtues that are most esteemed by the other players. You will receive a Predictions Form for this guess.

During the game, players meet in pairs (no meetings of three or more) to discuss the virtues. Although truth is one of the seven virtues, there is no rule that everyone must speak the truth the whole time, nor do players have to reveal the exact truth about their own personal values and emotions.

Write your name on your Identity Card plus the virtue you could discuss most freely. This may or may not be one of the virtues that you think you might vote for.

On your Meetings Form write down the name of each person you meet plus the virtue they would like to talk about.

Each meeting should discuss the emotions that people associate with the seven virtues and how they are regarded.

Finally, you should fill in your Predictions Form giving, in ranking order, the three virtues that you think the other players are most likely to vote for. The player whose Predictions Form most closely matches the actual result of the vote is the winner.

If your top choice is first you score three points, two points if it is second and one point if it is third.

In addition, you receive two points for any of your other guesses which are in the right order and one point if it is in the wrong order. For example, if your third choice comes third you score two points, but if it comes first or second you score one point.

The winner is the player who scores the most points.

Meetings Form

Person met	Virtues discussed	Comments

Predictions Form		
Name:		
I predict that the virtues will be ranked by everyone as follows:		
First:		
Second:		
Third:		
Virtue	Scores (votes)	Actual ranking order
Beauty		
Charity		
Faith		
Hope		
Humour		
Justice		
Truth		

Identity Cards – cut out

Name:	Name:
Let's talk about the virtue of:	*Let's talk about the virtue of:*
Name:	**Name:**
Let's talk about the virtue of:	*Let's talk about the virtue of:*
Name:	**Name:**
Let's talk about the virtue of:	*Let's talk about the virtue of:*
Name:	**Name:**
Let's talk about the virtue of:	*Let's talk about the virtue of:*

Virtue Cards – cut out

Beauty	**Charity**
Faith	**Hope**
Humour	**Justice**
Truth	

12 Boat Tax

Facilitator's Notes

DESCRIPTION

The time is hundreds of years ago. A tribe has introduced currency to replace barter. The highest piece of currency is a blue stone. The tribe levies a monthly tax of one blue stone on every working person and a yearly tax of two blue stones on the use of boats more than four paces in length. A meeting of the tribe has been called by protesters on the grounds that the boat tax is unfair to the fishcatchers.

At the meeting four of the groups have trades – arrowsmiths, potters, garmentmakers and hutbuilders. The fifth group do casual work and they are the ones who have called the meeting in protest against the boat tax. A sixth group are the Writers of Records in charge of the meeting.

No fishcatcher is present at the meeting. They have refused to attend because they work in the evening, which is when the meeting is being held.

AIMS

To reveal the sort of emotions associated with protest and vested interests.

COMMENTS

This simulation is easy to run. The rules of procedure are straightforward and only the person holding the round stone is allowed to speak.

TIME AND NUMBERS

The minimum number of participants is 12 – two for each of the five groups, plus two Writers of Records. Allow an hour for the event, but longer if you have a large number of participants.

MATERIALS

- Notes for Participants – one for each participant
- Law of the Tribe – one copy for each group
- Song of the Fishcatchers – one copy for each group
- Identity Cards – one for each participant

© Ken Jones, *Emotional Games for Training*, Gower Publishing Limited, 2002

- Six Knowledge Cards – one card for each group
- A round stone – not too heavy, yet sufficiently large that it cannot be concealed in the hand

BRIEFING

Before the event photocopy the materials for participants and cut out the required number of Identity and Knowledge Cards.

Hand out the Notes for Participants and discuss the mechanics of the simulation – the timing, the group areas, the area for the meeting of the tribe and possibly areas for leisurely breaks and private negotiations.

Retrieve the Notes for Participants and remove any non-tribal clutter from the area.

Place the Identity Cards face down and let the participants pick one each. They can then divide into their six groups – Arrowsmiths, Potters, Garmentmakers, Hutbuilders, Casual Workers and Writers of Records.

Hand out to each group a copy of the Law of the Tribe, the Song of the Fishcatchers, and the appropriate Knowledge Card.

Give the round stone to the Writers of Records.

ACTION

The simulation should run itself. The Writers of Records are in charge of the meeting and the procedures are simple and straightforward.

If you are asked questions about the mechanics of the event you can answer them or refer the questioner to the Writers of Records. If you are asked a question of fact – for example, 'How many fishcatchers are there?' or 'What is the total revenue in blue stones?' – then say that you don't know or that you are not a member of the tribe.

DEBRIEFING

Allow each group to debrief itself. When the groups come together they should first reveal what is written on their Knowledge Cards.

The emotions aroused may depend on the extent to which individual participants put themselves in the role of a person in an ancient tribe. Did they feel the mystique of the Law of the Tribe? Did they try to respect the traditions of the tribe? Did their behaviour and language match the situation in which they found themselves?

Most participants will probably have felt some degree of both group loyalty and tribal loyalty. A key question is what were their feelings about the Song of the Fishcatchers.

If necessary, you could point out that the situation arose because of the tribe's failure to envisage or consider the feelings of the fishcatchers.

Boat Tax: Notes for Participants

The time is hundreds of years ago. A tribe has introduced currency to replace barter. The highest piece of currency is a blue stone and the tribe levies a monthly tax of one blue stone on every working person and a yearly tax of two blue stones on the use of boats more than four paces in length. A meeting of the tribe has been called by protesters on the grounds that the boat tax is unfair to the fishcatchers.

By tradition, tribal meetings are held in the evening because that is the most convenient time for most of the tribe. Unfortunately it is also the time when fishcatchers work, so they only attend when the weather is stormy. They did not attend when it was decided to levy the Boat Tax. Almost immediately, the fishcatchers stopped using such boats in order to avoid the tax. Instead, they used smaller boats, and this resulted in not only less fish being caught but also more deaths at sea.

A meeting of the tribe has been called by the casual workers who often help bring fish ashore. They are protesting against the tax on the grounds that it is unfair to the fishcatchers. You will be a member of one of six groups at this meeting. Four groups have regular trades – arrowsmiths, potters, garmentmakers and hutbuilders. A fifth group comprises the casual workers and the sixth group are the Writers of Records in charge of the meeting.

The fishcatchers have refused to attend in protest against the tax and the fact that the meeting is being held at a time when they catch fish. You will receive a copy of the Song of the Fishcatchers which sets out their grievances.

You will also have a copy of the Law of the Tribe, setting out the procedures for the meeting, and each group will have a Knowledge Card which sets out the group's current thinking. However, these attitudes can be modified as a result of what is said at the meeting and in private discussions with other members of the tribe.

© Ken Jones, *Emotional Games for Training*, Gower Publishing Limited, 2002

LAW OF THE TRIBE

This is the law of the tribe.

The highest law is loyalty to the tribe.

The Round Stone represents the unity of the tribe.

When the tribe meets to discuss law they must use the Round Stone.

Under the law, only the person holding the Round Stone may speak. They that are without the Round Stone may not speak.

The Stone must pass round the tribe so that everyone can have a chance to speak and show loyalty to the tribe and the law of the tribe.

The Writers of the Records are in charge of the law of the tribe. They are the guardians of the unity of the tribe and are the keepers of the Round Stone. They are in charge of the meetings of the tribe and start the meeting by holding the Round Stone.

The Writers of the Records keep a record of any vote, but they themselves may not vote.

SONG OF THE FISHCATCHERS

We are the catchers of fish. Our boats are no longer than four paces because of the tax.

We are the catchers of fish. Our catches are small because our boats are small because of the tax.

We are the catchers of fish. Our living is poor because our catches are small because of the tax.

We are the catchers of fish. We have to keep fishing and we die in rough seas because of the tax.

Identity Cards – cut out

Arrowsmiths	**Garmentmakers**
Hutbuilders	**Potters**
Casual workers	**Writers of Records**

Knowledge Cards – cut out

Arrowsmiths' knowledge

Some members of the tribe may think it would be a good idea to put a tax on arrows. But arrows are essential for the hunters. The tribe needs food. If the price of arrows goes up, then so will the price of food. This would cause hardship to poor people.
    Would it not be a good idea to levy a tax on the size and number of huts? This would affect only those rich people who could afford to pay the tax. Some rich people have big huts, and some have more than one hut.

Garmentmakers' knowledge

Some members of the tribe may think it would be a good idea to put a tax on garments. But clothes are not a luxury; they are essential.
    If garments were taxed, it would hit the poor who would find clothes too expensive.
    Would it not be better to put a tax on pots? This would encourage people to take more care and not break so many pots.

© Ken Jones, *Emotional Games for Training*, Gower Publishing Limited, 2002

Knowledge Cards – continued

Hutmakers' knowledge

Some members of the tribe may think it would be a good idea to put a tax on huts. But huts are essential. Each member of the tribe should be able to have a strong hut for themselves and their family. Some people who hunt or farm or collect fruit have two huts because their work is away from the village. If huts were taxed, it would cause food prices to rise.

Some people who are poor need large huts for their families. If a tax were levied on the size of huts it would hit the poor.

Would it not be better to put a tax on garments? The wealthy have more garments than the poor.

Potters' knowledge

Some members of the tribe may think it would be a good idea to put a tax on pots. They might think that this would make people take more care not to break so many pots. But, however careful people are, pots get broken in the heat of the fire.

Pots are essential for cooking. Poor people would be hit by a tax on pots. Many poor people have large families and need more pots than wealthy people with small families.

Would it not be better to put a tax on arrows? Wealthy people use arrows for sport.

Knowledge Cards – continued

Casual workers' knowledge

The Boat Tax is unfair not only because it damages the fishcatchers, but also because it was decided at a meeting when no fishcatcher was present.

We should look for other times to hold meetings.

Fishing is an important trade for the tribe, and it was a mistake to impose the tax. The tribe should agree that we made a mistake and the tax should be abolished.

A tax should be levied on people who have goods – on their arrows, pots, garments and huts. This would be fair as poor people, who own fewer goods, would be the least affected.

Writers of Records' knowledge

We are the guardians of the Round Stone. We write the records, we are the keepers of the Law and we are in charge of meetings that discuss law.

If some members of the tribe think it unfair that all meetings are held at the time that the sun goes down, then let that proposal be put forward. It is not a matter for us; it is a matter for the tribe.

If some members of the tribe think that the Boat Tax should be replaced by a tax on arrows or pots or garments or huts, then let such proposals be put forward and let each speak as they feel. It is not a matter for us; it is a matter for the tribe.

We talk among ourselves before we talk to the tribe so that we may say nothing that is not agreed between us.

We have no vote, but we are members of the tribe and we can have our say.

13 Hunting Pink

Facilitator's Notes

DESCRIPTION

A simulation set in the offices of South Alpha Culture involving the design of an event called Hunting Pink in which there are three groups – Huntsmen, Huntswomen and Foxes. The foxes may also hunt and win if they outnumber the hunters. Huntsmen can hunt huntswomen and vice versa.

In order to get into the feel of the game the designers are divided into three groups – Huntsmen, Huntswomen and Foxes – to devise rules that would be useful and acceptable to participants in that role.

AIMS

To reveal the sort of emotions related to high-profile issues such as hunting and sexual competition.

COMMENTS

Some care should be taken if the participants include both sexes. As with any event which involves males and females in direct competition, it is vital to make sure that everyone is willing to participate. Participants should be given the option of taking on the role of observer or of being an Executive of South Alpha Culture.

At the end of the event some participants may request that they be allowed to play the version of the game they have just devised, but not everyone may be happy with this suggestion.

TIME AND NUMBERS

The minimum number of participants is six – two in each team – and there is no maximum number. Allow between one and two hours, depending on how many people take part.

MATERIALS

- Notes for Participants – one for each participant
- Memo – one for each participant
- Suggestions for Huntsmen, Huntswomen and Foxes – one for each member of the appropriate team
- Rule Forms – one for each of the teams
- Identity Cards for the three roles – one card for each participant

BRIEFING

Before the event photocopy the materials for participants and cut out the required number of Identity Cards.

Hand out the Notes for Participants. Discuss the mechanics of the event – the timing and the location of the teams.

Retrieve the Notes for Participants and remove any clutter that would not normally be found in the offices of South Alpha Culture.

Place the Identity Cards face down and allow the participants to pick their own. Then divide into three groups – Huntsmen, Huntswomen and Foxes.

Hand out the Memo – one to each participant.

Hand out the Suggestions – one to each member of the appropriate team.

Hand out the Rule Forms – one to each team.

ACTION

Once the three groups have been formed, the simulation will run itself.

If you have one or two participants in the role of Directors of South Alpha Culture they can deal with queries. For example, you or they might be asked whether there are any horses on the estate.

If you are asked factual questions you could say that you don't know the answer or, if it is a very important issue, you could say that you will fax the organizers in Milan – in which case the information should be given to all the teams.

DEBRIEFING

The event ends with the three groups meeting together so, if the participants have not already done so, they can put everyone in the picture regarding the questions that were suggested to the group at the beginning of the event.

There are two emotional levels: first, the actual emotions of the participants during the action; and, second, the imaginary emotions that might be felt by the participants during the Milan event.

As suggested earlier, the emotions may become volatile and, in such circumstances, you must try to defuse the situation and avoid people being offended.

Try to make sure that the discussion focuses mainly on the design aspects and does not become sidetracked into heated arguments about how men treat women and vice versa.

Consider what you should do if some participants request that they be allowed to play the game they have designed.

Hunting Pink: Notes for Participants

You are members of South Alpha Culture, an organization that designs games and simulations for corporate clients.

You have been asked to design a game called Hunting Pink to be run at the start of a four-day conference of international property dealers in Milan. The idea is that the game would act as an international icebreaker and help social mix.

In Hunting Pink there will be three groups – Huntsmen, Huntswomen and Foxes. The foxes can also hunt and win if they outnumber the hunters. Huntsmen can hunt huntswomen and vice versa.

In order to get into the feel of the game, the designers are divided into three groups – Huntsmen, Huntswomen and Foxes – to devise rules that would be useful and acceptable to participants in that role.

The situation is explained in a memo from the Managing Director of South Alpha Culture.

South Alpha
CULTURE

Memo

From: Managing Director

To: Design Teams

We have been commissioned to produce a game for an international conference of property dealers which will take place in the summer near Milan. The idea is to devise a game to encourage social mix at the start of the conference.

About 50 players are likely to participate. The venue is the estate of a well-known winery. There is a large villa on the estate containing public rooms, private rooms, a music room, games room and library as well as accommodation for about 30 participants. Other participants will be housed in converted farm buildings in the grounds of the estate. The grounds include gardens, swimming pool, tennis courts, lake (with a few boats) and small summer houses. The estate's vineyards surround the villa and gardens.

We have agreed with the organizers of the conference that the game will be called Hunting Pink and the participants will be huntsmen, huntswomen and foxes. The foxes may capture any huntsmen or huntswomen if they outnumber them. Any of the three groups can hunt any other group.

About a quarter of the players are likely to be women. Some of the women will be property dealers; others will be the men's wives or partners.

We realize that playing this game might provide strong emotions so I want you to divide randomly into three groups – Huntsmen, Huntswomen and Foxes – and devise rules that would make the event interesting (and relatively safe) from the point of view of players who are in that particular role.

You will be given Identity Cards so that individuals can visit other groups and exchange ideas. We will also give each team a list of suggestions relating to their particular role. The purpose is not to give you answers, but to raise questions.

One important consideration – we want the event to be fully participatory. The aim of encouraging social mix will not be achieved if anyone is eliminated in the first five minutes and has to stand around waiting for the others to finish.

Finally, you should all meet together (as design experts) and see if you can come up with some useful rules for the game.

Good luck!

South Alpha
CULTURE

Milan Conference – Hunting Pink game

SUGGESTIONS FOR HUNTSMEN

Since this is the first event of the conference it is important that the rules should uphold dignity – few of these players will be young people. Perhaps there could be a no-touch rule, or capture could merely be a touch on the arm.

How should the participants be allocated roles? Should all the women be in the role of huntswomen, all the men be huntsmen and the foxes be a mixed group? Or should roles be allocated at random?

What should constitute a successful hunt? If three huntsmen successfully ambushed two huntswomen, would the women be captured and what should happen next?

The rules must specify what areas are available for play. For example, can Huntsman Romeo invite Huntswoman Juliet into his bedroom or vice versa?

What tokens, instructions, artefacts or identity cards would be required?

South Alpha
CULTURE

Milan Conference – Hunting Pink game

SUGGESTIONS FOR HUNTSWOMEN

Should roles be allocated at random? This might lead to embarrassment – for example, men could end up in the role of huntswomen.

Many of the female participants may feel vulnerable. Instead of concentrating on hunting foxes they may feel at risk from males – both from the huntsmen and the male foxes. Conversely, it is equally possible that some women may relish a situation in which they can hunt males.

It may be a good idea to give the huntswomen one or two bases in which they are safe – perhaps the library or music room, for example.

Participants, particularly the huntswomen, need protection from physical contact. The chances of bodily injury, or claims of physical assault or sexual harassment, should be minimized.

A key feature is to decide what constitutes a successful hunt. Should the rules of capture be the same for the three groups? Should it be easier for huntswomen to make a capture? Should running be prohibited? Should huntsmen have to walk backwards all the time? What happens in the event of a successful capture? Clearly, the captured player cannot be simply eliminated from the game.

Perhaps bottles of wine, or grapes or the concept of property could feature in the game. Would identity cards or artefacts be useful?

South Alpha
CULTURE

Milan Conference – Hunting Pink game

SUGGESTIONS FOR FOXES

People in the role of foxes are likely to consider fox-like qualities – cunning and stealth. So they might consider disguise, ambushes and secret alliances with other groups. Should any of these tactics be prohibited by the rules? Should resources (for example, masks) be provided to facilitate such tactics?

It would be unfair if foxes did not have equal status with the other groups. This might be done by having half the participants in the role of foxes and a quarter each in the other two groups. Otherwise it might be difficult for the foxes to reach a position where they outnumber another group.

Perhaps it would be a good idea for the foxes to have security status in several different bases (earths) – perhaps the summer houses.

Should physical contact be permitted between hunters and the hunted? What should signify capture?

Should everyone have identity cards with perhaps a few spare cards if capture were to be followed by possible recruitment?

What should be the rules for the captured? Should they lose points? Should they have to drink a glass of wine before they could resume? Should they have the option of changing roles and joining the successful hunter?

South Alpha CULTURE

Milan Conference – Hunting Pink game

Rule Form

1.

2.

3.

4.

5.

6.

7.

8.

9.

10.

Identity Cards – cut out

Huntsman Name:	Huntswoman Name:	Fox Name:
Huntsman Name:	Huntswoman Name:	Fox Name:
Huntsman Name:	Huntswoman Name:	Fox Name:

14 Elite

Facilitator's Notes

DESCRIPTION

The first two international exchange students from the Republic of Omega are due to arrive at the Central Training College in the Republic of Alpha. Both are from a racial group called Elits and, in Omega, it is taken for granted that their average intelligence is higher than the average of the rest of the population.

There are roles for Alpha Television and four groups at the Training College – Governors, Administrators, Faculty and Students' Union.

Note: because racial discrimination is such a sensitive issue it is important to check that everyone is willing to participate. Show copies of the Notes for Participants to the potential participants before attempting to run this event and, during the simulation, be ready to offer a change of role for anyone who becomes distressed.

AIMS

To reveal the sort of emotions associated with negotiations about human rights and the controversial subjects of intelligence and race.

COMMENTS

It could be useful to recruit an assistant facilitator to help in arranging the initiatives of the five groups – Alpha Television, Governors, Administrators, Faculty and Students' Union. This could include organizing the time and place for news conferences, arranging for the participants to stop work and attend, and arranging for the publication of news items and statements.

TIME AND NUMBERS

The minimum number is ten participants – two in the role of Alpha Television and four pairs representing the four groups in the Training College. There is no maximum number. Allow two hours for the event.

MATERIALS

- Notes for Participants – one for each participant
- A cutting from the *Alpha Times* – one for each participant

- Alpha Central Training College Procedures – one for each group
- Extract from a document issued by the Republic of Omega's Ministry of Information – one for each participant
- Alpha Central College Procedures – one for each group
- Five Knowledge Cards – one for each group (Governors, Administrators, Faculty, Students' Union and Alpha Television)
- Identity Cards – one for each participant in each group

BRIEFING

Before the event, photocopy the materials for participants and cut out the required number of Knowledge and Identity Cards.

Hand out the Notes for Participants. Check that everyone is willing to participate.

Discuss the mechanics of the event – timing, the location of the groups, the arrangements for news conferences and publishing, plus facilities – perhaps microphone, videocamera, flipcharts, and so on.

Place the Identity Cards face downwards and let everyone pick their own. When they have divided into their groups, retrieve the Notes for Participants and remove any clutter that would not be present in the locations.

Hand out to each group the other public materials:

- the cutting from the *Alpha Times* – one for each participant
- Extract from the document issued by the Republic of Omega's Ministry of Information – one for each participant
- Alpha Central College Procedures – one for each group.

Then hand out the Knowledge Cards to the appropriate groups.

ACTION

The simulation will run better if you appoint an assistant facilitator to look after the resources and timing of group initiatives. This includes the arrangements for passing of messages from one group to another.

If you want to include breaks, they are best taken after news conferences or meetings so that participants have an opportunity to digest what has been said and discuss the developing situation.

DEBRIEFING

It is a good idea for each group to hold its own mini-debriefing to discuss the most interesting or important aspects of the event and to consider individual emotions, group emotions and the perceived emotions of other groups. Give each group a copy of the Emotional

Word List (or your own selection) to help them assess the behaviour of themselves and others.

One of the advantages of having a mini-debriefing is that it should help the participants to detach from the immediate emotions of the event and become more dispassionate. They no longer need to assume that 'Our side was right.'

The subsequent main debriefing could begin with each group revealing what was on their Knowledge Card and then explaining what they did and why they did it.

Important note: as mentioned earlier, race is a sensitive issue so it is just as important to prevent people from becoming upset during the debriefing as it was during the simulation itself. Try to confine the discussion to the specific situation in Alpha and avoid ranging over worldwide racial problems.

Should there be signs of antagonism developing between participants, revert to the mini-debriefing mode to allow tempers to cool and dispassion to reappear.

Elite: Notes for Participants

The first two international exchange students from the Republic of Omega are due to arrive at the Central Training College in the Republic of Alpha. Both are from a racial group called Elits. The media in Alpha tend to call them 'Elites'.

A cutting from the *Alpha Times* reports on the current situation and some of the background information can be found in the document from the Omega Ministry of Information. You will also receive a document setting out the procedures at the Central Training College, particularly regarding contact with official bodies.

You will be divided randomly into five groups – Governors, Administrators, Faculty, Students' Union and Alpha Television.

Each group will receive its own Knowledge Card giving the group's immediate perception of the situation. The Knowledge Cards are not supposed to exist as such, so do not show your Card to other groups. However, the knowledge is not confidential, and you can reveal it.

It is your task to represent your group's interests in the best way you can – by sending messages to other groups, by meeting other groups, by giving news conferences and by being interviewed by Alpha TV.

Do not invent 'facts' – the only facts are in the documents. If questioned at interviews (or at meetings) you can invent explanations, but only if they are plausible and probable extensions of the facts.

Although you may have strong personal views, try to stay in role and work within the consensus of your own group. Confine your discussions and action to the situation in the Training College.

Participation in this event is entirely voluntary. If you would prefer not to take part or would like to change to another role, then have a word with the facilitator.

ALPHA TIMES
Hostile reception awaits two Elites
Central College in turmoil as students threaten to riot

For the first time ever, two Elite students from the Republic of Omega are due to arrive in Alpha where they have been enrolled at the Central Training College. They face a stormy reception because they are both members of the top race in Omega whose members hold most of the important jobs in that country. The students at the College claim that to accept the Elites is to condone racism.

Yesterday, students waving placards saying 'Elites go home' and '"No to racism"' staged a small demonstration at the College. Larger demonstrations are expected when the Elites arrive tomorrow. The two students were chosen in a competition open to students in Omega and both have said that they are pleased to be chosen to come to Alpha.

The situation will be discussed at meetings of the Governors, the Administration, the teachers and the students.

Our political correspondent writes:

The Charter of the College states that the authorities must 'provide an education free from discrimination by gender, race, creed or religion'. In Omega, Elits (they are not called 'Elites' in Omega) tend to go to the best schools and get the best jobs. Although people of Caucasian, Asian and African origin account for 80 per cent of the population, it is estimated that more than half the politicians, administrators and executives are Elits. Professor Redling of North Alpha University says, 'Although in Omega it is assumed that the Elits are more intelligent, this may simply mean that they are better at scoring highly in intelligence tests. However, Omega has a culture based on tolerance and there are laws prohibiting racial discrimination.'

ALPHA CENTRAL TRAINING COLLEGE
College Procedures

The Board of Governors feels that it may be helpful to set out the various procedures designed to encourage friendly contact between groups within the College and also procedures when dealing with the media.

The College upholds a tradition of open democratic and civilized behaviour. Thus, if one group has a complaint about another group, the complaint should be first raised with the group concerned.

However, if the matter is not a complaint then any group is perfectly free to approach the media.

In order to ensure orderly discussion between College groups, meetings should take place only by prior mutual agreement – thus, one person may visit, or send a message to, another College group, requesting a meeting.

If group statements are to be issued, either in writing or in interviews with the media, then other groups should be informed in advance – although this does not imply any right of veto or censorship.

The Board of Governors firmly believes that the media should be considered to be fair and friendly rather than hostile and unfriendly.

REPUBLIC OF OMEGA
Ministry of Information

On the issues of racism and discrimination

Various sections of the foreign media have consistently, over many years, accused the Government of the Republic of Omega of discrimination and racism.

In reply, the Omegan Government has always denied that there is any racial discrimination practised by any official body in Omega. The facts are as follows.

1. Racial discrimination is outlawed by the Constitution and several specific Acts of Parliament state that discrimination by race, gender or age is illegal in areas such as employment, education, recruitment and accommodation.
2. In the Omegan language the word 'Elit' refers to a separate race of people inhabiting the Uplands in the north. It does not mean 'elite' as reported in the foreign media. Elits are a minority within a multicultural society, including people of European, Asian and African descent.
3. In the long history of Omega the leaders in almost all fields – government, business, art, economics and science – have mostly been ethnic Elits and it is generally accepted by all the races in Omega that Elits are more intelligent and that their presence is a great national asset. But there is no definite proof that the Elits are intellectually superior. No 'intelligent gene' has been found.
4. There are many theories – that the Elits are the only survivors of an ancient race, or that they are the descendants of a group of space travellers, or that they are a long-lost tribe that migrated to Omega in prehistoric times. No one knows.
5. All jobs within government, and most jobs within industry, are based on open competition. There is no discrimination in favour of the Elits. On several occasions, the Omegan Government has considered introducing positive discrimination in favour of non-Elits but this has always been rejected on the grounds that the interests of the country is best served by being a meritocracy.
6. The Government considers that any international discrimination against Elits is undemocratic, a denial of their rights as human beings and an affront to the national dignity of Omega.

Knowledge Cards – cut out

Governors' knowledge

The Governors will, at all times, abide by the law of the Republic of Alpha.

The Charter of the Central Training College states that the Governors 'shall at all times act in accordance with the best interests of the College and provide an education free from discrimination by gender, race, creed or religion'.

There is nothing illegal about the entry of these two Elit students into this country. In fact, there are several hundred Elits in Alpha working in connection with trade. However, the main obligation of the Governors is to act in the best interests of the College. This means that each situation should be examined on its merits.

We hope to learn more about the views of the Administration, the Faculty and the Students' Union with regard to this matter.

Administrators' knowledge

The two Elit students have paid for their one-year course and we accepted their enrolment in the same way as we admit all students, both from home and abroad, who show sufficient evidence of attainment to justify the belief that they will benefit from our courses.

The two students have excellent qualifications. They fully accept the requirement to obey the College regulations and also the law of the land.

We could have refused them admission had they been criminals or intent on causing trouble, but this was not the case. They have committed no crime, they are suitable for the course and they should be admitted.

Knowledge Cards – continued

Faculty knowledge

We are not happy about the admission of the two Elit students as we believe they may, through no fault of their own, become a cause of disruption – possibly serious disruption. This would almost certainly lead to problems in teaching and have an adverse effect on academic standards and examination results.

Our students, and some of our own staff, openly object to the racial culture of Omega and will doubtless wish to show their displeasure. This is a dangerous situation which could seriously damage the reputation of the College.

We have no wish to see police called to the campus. We are concerned for the safety of both students and staff.

Students' Union knowledge

We oppose all elitist and reactionary regimes.

We are seriously concerned that accepting the two Elite students will be seen as support for elitism, racism and privilege. We shall not be organizing demonstrations, but undoubtedly there will be demonstrations. Even peaceful demonstrations may get out of hand. We are aware of the possibility that any demonstrations could be infiltrated by political and social extremists from outside the College who are dedicated to violence.

One solution would be for the Elite students to be sent back home and replaced by two students of other races – Europeans, Asians or Africans. Alternatively, most of our members might be willing to accept four students from Omega – one Elite, and three non-Elites – giving a better representation of the population of Omega.

Knowledge Cards – continued

Alpha Television knowledge

Our job in Alpha Television is to broadcast news and comment. The imminent arrival of the two so-called elite students at the Central Training College is a matter of considerable public interest. This is confirmed by the fact that the *Alpha Times* ran the story on its front page today.

We must contact all the four groups involved – Governors, Administrators, Faculty and representatives of the Students' Union.

Our usual format is a news report followed by one or more interviews. However, the format is flexible and can be adapted according to circumstances.

Race is a sensitive issue and we must remember that our Licence to Broadcast contains a commitment on our part to aim for fair, open and unprejudiced reporting.

It is our job to be impartial. It is also our job to get the news and report it.

Identity Cards – cut out

Governor Name:	**Administrator** Name:
Faculty Name:	**Student's Union** Name:
Alpha Television Name:	

15 Way Out

Facilitator's Notes

DESCRIPTION

An advertising agency – Alpha Promotions Inc. – has invited university graduates to apply for jobs in its Editorial Department. Part of the selection procedure comprises a test to invent and promote a fictional product that could be described as 'way out'.

AIMS

To reveal the sort of emotions involved in creating, presenting and evaluating extreme ideas.

COMMENTS

There are roles for Executives of the advertising agency and Graduates. The procedures are fairly straightforward, so there should be few problems in running the event.

TIME AND NUMBERS

The minimum number of participants is eight – two Executives and six Graduates. There is no maximum number. With small numbers allow approximately an hour; with larger numbers, up to two hours.

MATERIALS

- Notes for Participants – one copy for each participant
- Test Instructions – one copy for each participant
- Project Form – one copy for each of the Graduates
- Assessment Form – one copy for each of the Executives
- Identity Cards – one for each participant
- Resources for presentations – coloured pens, paper, cards, flipcharts, and so on

BRIEFING

Before the event photocopy the materials for participants and cut out the required number of Identity Cards.

Hand out the Notes for Participants and discuss the mechanics of the simulation. Try to allow ample space for the meetings to take place in reasonable privacy. It may be advisable to set time limits for the stages of the various meetings and the presentations.

Retrieve the Notes for Participants and remove any clutter that would not be normally present in the test situation.

Hand out the Test Instructions – one to each participant.

Use the Identity Cards to divide the participants into their two categories – Executives and Graduates. Give each of the Executives an Assessment Form and each Graduate a Project Form.

Discuss the resources that might be used for the presentations. Could music or costumes be made available for dramatic scenes? Could members of other groups be recruited for crowd scenes?

ACTION

The simulation should run itself, but the nature of the presentations will depend on ideas generated during the course of the test.

DEBRIEFING

Allow the different groups, including the Executives, to debrief themselves and then explain to the other groups what they felt about what they did and what other groups did.

Was any group particularly pleased with itself? Did any groups engage in drama for the presentations and how did they feel about this?

Did anyone feel that some of the way-out ideas were becoming more plausible and how did this affect their emotions?

Way Out: Notes for Participants

An advertising agency – Alpha Promotions Inc. – has invited university graduates to apply for jobs in its Editorial Department as part of an expansion of its activities.

Part of the selection process involves a test to invent a fictional product that could be described as 'way out' and then to present the idea to the Executives and the other Graduates as plausibly and spectacularly as possible.

The situation is described in the Test Instructions.

You will be either an Executive of the company or one of the Graduates being tested for the job.

ALPHA PROMOTIONS INC.

TEST INSTRUCTIONS

This test is to see whether you can free yourself of any academic discipline that might inhibit your development into a top advertising executive.

Your task is to invent a product that could be described as 'way out'. If you can't think of a suitable idea, then invent a special Cat's Whisker Comb to be sold to the owners of pet cats.

You start the test by individually thinking of one or two preliminary ideas which you enter on your Project Form.

Then you meet in pairs – three meetings of three minutes each with other graduates. You are then free to meet others to develop ideas. You can form groups or work as individuals.

Keep filling in your Project Form as you develop or change your earlier ideas.

The test is concluded with a presentation of your 'way out' project to the executives and the other graduates.

If you have decided to work alone on your project, you can ask other graduates to help you with your presentation.

If you work in pairs then you are allowed to present two ideas if you wish. Similarly a group of three could present one, two or three projects.

The presentations should aim to be creative, not routine, explanations. You can use drama whenever appropriate. You can use any of the facilities available. Think in terms of advertising campaigns and showbusiness.

Good luck!

ALPHA PROMOTIONS INC.

Project Form

Name:

Early ideas:

Later ideas, including presentation:

Alpha Promotions Inc.

Assessment Form

Name:

Name of presenter	Comments on ideas, style and innovation

Identity Cards – cut out

Graduate Name:	**Graduate** Name:
Graduate Name:	**Graduate** Name:
Graduate Name:	**Graduate** Name:
Executive Name:	**Executive** Name:

Other works by Ken Jones

Games and Simulations Made Easy, London: Kogan Page, 1997.
Creative Events for Trainers, Maidenhead: McGraw-Hill, 1997.
Icebreakers, London: Kogan Page, 1995.
Simulations in Language Teaching, Cambridge: Cambridge University Press, 1982.